BY THE RIVER PIEDRA
I SAT DOWN AND WEPT

PAULO COELHO

BY THE RIVER PIEDRA
I SAT DOWN AND WEPT

TRANSLATED BY ALAN R. CLARKE

HarperCollins*Publishers*

By the River Piedra I Sat Down and Wept is an English version of
Na margem do rio Piedra eu sentei e chorei, the Portugese original
edition, published in Brazil by Editora Rocca Ltd (Rio de Janeiro),
copyright © 1994 by Paulo Coelho.
English translation by Alan R. Clarke.

HarperCollins*Publishers*
77–85 Fulham Palace Road,
Hammersmith, London W6 8JB

HarperCollins website address is:
www.harpercollins.co.uk
Paulo Coelho's website address is:
http://www.paulocoelho.com.br

Original hardback English translation published
by HarperSanFrancisco 1996
Paperback edition published by
HarperCollins 1997, 1999
This edition published 2005

1 3 5 7 9 8 6 4 2

© English translation HarperCollins Publishers Inc. 1996

Paulo Coelho asserts the moral right to be
identified as the author of this work

A catalogue record for this book
is available from the British Library

ISBN 0 0077 3695 9

Printed and bound in China by Imago

For I. C. and S. B., whose loving communion made me see the feminine face of God;

for Monica Antunes, my companion from the beginning, who with her love and enthusiasm spreads the fire all over the world;

for Paulo Rocco, for the joy of the battles we have fought together and for the dignity of the battles we have fought between us;

and for Matthew Lore, for not having forgotten a sage quotation from the I Ching: "Perseverance is favorable."

Author's Note

A Spanish missionary was visiting an island when he came across three Aztec priests.

"How do you pray?" the missionary asked.

"We have only one prayer," answered one of the Aztecs. "We say, 'God, you are three, we are three. Have pity on us.'"

"A beautiful prayer," said the missionary. "But it is not exactly the one that God heeds. I'm going to teach you one that's much better."

The padre taught them a Catholic prayer and then continued on his path of evangelism. Years later, when he was returning to Spain, his ship stopped again at the island. From the deck, the missionary saw the three priests on the shore and waved to them.

Just then, the three men began to walk across the water toward him.

"Padre! Padre!" one of them called, approaching the ship. "Teach us again that prayer that God heeds. We've forgotten how it goes."

"It doesn't matter," responded the missionary, witnessing the miracle. And he promptly asked God's forgiveness for failing to recognize that He speaks all languages.

This story illustrates just what this book is about. Rarely do we realize that we are in the midst of the extraordinary. Miracles occur all around us, signs from God show us the way, angels plead to be heard, but we pay little attention to them because we have been taught that we must follow certain formulas and rules if we want to find God. We do not recognize that God is wherever we allow Him/Her to enter.

Traditional religious practices are important: they allow us to share with others the communal experience of adoration and prayer. But we must never forget that spiritual experience is above all a *practical* experience of love. And with love, there are no rules. Some may try to control their emotions and develop strategies for their behavior; others may turn to reading books of advice from "experts" on relationships—but this is all folly. The heart decides, and what it decides is all that really matters.

All of us have had this experience. At some point, we have each said through our tears, "I'm suffering for a love that's not worth it." We suffer because we feel we are giving more than we receive. We suffer because our love is going unrecognized. We suffer because we are unable to impose our own rules.

But ultimately there is no good reason for our suffering, for in every love lies the seed of our growth. The more we love, the closer we come to spiritual experience. Those who are truly enlightened, those whose souls are illuminated by love, have been able to overcome all of the inhibitions and preconceptions of their era. They have been able to sing, to laugh, and to pray out loud; they have danced and shared what Saint Paul called "the madness of saintliness." They have been joyful—because those who love conquer the world and have no fear of loss. True love is an act of total surrender.

This book is about the importance of that surrender. Pilar and her companion are fictitious, but they represent the many conflicts that beset us in our search for love. Sooner or later, we have to overcome our fears, because the spiritual path can only be traveled through the daily experience of love.

Thomas Merton once said that the spiritual life is essentially to love. One doesn't love in order to do what is good or to help or to protect someone. If we act that way, we are perceiving the other as a simple object, and we are seeing ourselves as wise and generous persons. This has nothing to do with love. To love is to be in communion with the other and to discover in that other the spark of God.

May Pilar's lament on the bank of the River Piedra guide us toward such communion.

Paulo Coelho

ɕ *ɕ* *ɕ*

But wisdom is justified
by all her children.

Luke 7:35

By the River Piedra
I Sat Down and Wept

ᕯ ᕯ ᕯ

BY THE RIVER Piedra
I sat down and wept.
There is a legend that everything that falls into the waters of this river—leaves, insects, the feathers of birds—is transformed into the rocks that make the riverbed.
If only I could tear out my heart and hurl it into the current, then my pain and longing would be over, and
I could finally forget.

By the River Piedra I sat down and wept. The winter air chills the tears on my cheeks, and my tears fall into the cold waters that course past me. Somewhere, this river joins another, then another, until—far from my heart and sight—all of them merge with the sea.

May my tears run just as far, that my love might never know that one day I cried for him. May my tears run just as far, that I might forget the River Piedra, the monastery, the church in the Pyrenees, the mists, and the paths we walked together.

I shall forget the roads, the mountains, and the fields of my dreams—the dreams that will never come true.

I remember my "magic moment"—that instant when a "yes" or a "no" can change one's life forever. It seems so long ago now. It is hard to believe that it was only last week that I had found my love once again, and then lost him.

I am writing this story on the bank of the River Piedra. My hands are freezing, my legs are numb, and every minute I want to stop.

"Seek to live. Remembrance is for the old," he said.

Perhaps love makes us old before our time—or young, if youth has passed. But how can I not recall those moments? That is why I write—to try to turn sadness into longing, solitude into remembrance. So that when I finish telling myself the story, I can toss it into the Piedra. That's what the woman who has given me shelter told me to do. Only then—in the words of one of the saints—will the water extinguish what the flames have written.

All love stories are the same.

(› (› (›

W E HAD BEEN children together. Then he left, like so many young people who leave small towns. He said he was going to learn about the world, that his dreams lay beyond the fields of Soria.

Years passed with almost no news of him. Every now and then he would send me a letter, but he never returned to the paths and forests of our childhood.

When I finished school, I moved to Zaragoza, and there I found that he had been right. Soria *was* a small town, and as its only famous poet had said, roads are made to be traveled. I enrolled in the university and found a boyfriend. I began to study for a scholarship (I was working as a salesgirl to pay for my courses). But I lost the competition for the scholarship, and after that I left my boyfriend.

Then the letters from my childhood friend began to arrive more frequently—and I was envious of the stamps from so many different places. He seemed to know everything; he had sprouted wings, and now he roamed the world. Meanwhile, I was simply trying to put down roots.

Some of his letters, all mailed from the same place in France, spoke of God. In one, he wrote about wanting to enter a seminary and dedicate his life to prayer. I wrote him back, asking him to wait a bit, urging him to experience more of his freedom before committing himself to something so serious.

But after I reread my letter, I tore it up. Who was I to speak about freedom or commitment? Compared to him, I knew nothing about such things.

One day I learned that he had begun to give lectures. This surprised me; I thought he was too young to be able to teach anything to anyone. And then he wrote to me that he was going to speak to a small group in Madrid—and he asked me to come.

So I made the four-hour trip from Zaragoza to Madrid. I wanted to see him again; I wanted to hear his voice. I wanted to sit with him in a café and remember the old days, when we had thought the world was far too large for anyone ever to know it truly.

Saturday, December 4, 1993

❧ ❧ ❧

THE PLACE where the conference was held was more formal than I had imagined it, and there were more people there than I had expected. How had all this come about?

He must be famous, I thought. He'd said nothing about this in his letters. I wanted to go up to the people in the audience and ask them why they were there, but I didn't have the nerve.

I was even more surprised when I saw him enter the room. He was quite different from the boy I had known —but of course, it had been twelve years; people change. Tonight his eyes were shining—he looked wonderful.

"He's giving us back what was ours," said a woman seated next to me.

A strange thing to say.

"What is he giving back?" I asked.

"What was stolen from us. Religion."

"No, no, he's not giving us anything back," said a younger woman seated on my right. "They can't return something that has always belonged to us."

"Well, then, what are you doing here?" the first woman asked, irritated.

"I want to listen to him. I want to see how they think; they've already burned us at the stake once, and they may want to do it again."

"He's just one voice," said the woman. "He's doing what he can."

The young woman smiled sarcastically and turned away, putting an end to the conversation.

"He's taking a courageous position for a seminarian," the other woman went on, looking to me for support.

I didn't understand any of this, and I said nothing. The woman finally gave up. The girl at my side winked at me, as if I were her ally.

But I was silent for a different reason. I was thinking, *Seminarian? It can't be! He would have told me.*

When he started to speak, I couldn't concentrate. I was sure he had spotted me in the audience, and I was trying to guess what he was thinking. How did I look to him? How different was the woman of twenty-nine from the girl of seventeen?

I noticed that his voice hadn't changed. But his words certainly had.

❧ ❧ ❧

YOU HAVE TO take risks, he said. We will only understand the miracle of life fully when we allow the unexpected to happen.

Every day, God gives us the sun—and also one moment in which we have the ability to change everything that makes us unhappy. Every day, we try to pretend that we haven't perceived that moment, that it doesn't exist—that today is the same as yesterday and will be the same as tomorrow. But if people really pay attention to their everyday lives, they will discover that magic moment. It may arrive in the instant when we are doing something mundane, like putting our front-door key in the lock; it may lie hidden in the quiet that follows the lunch hour or in the thousand and one things that all seem the same to us. But that moment exists—a moment when all the power of the stars becomes a part of us and enables us to perform miracles.

Joy is sometimes a blessing, but it is often a conquest. Our magic moment helps us to change and sends us off in search of our dreams. Yes, we are going to suffer, we will have difficult times, and we will experience many disappointments—but all of this is transitory; it leaves no permanent mark. And one day we will look back with pride and faith at the journey we have taken.

Pitiful is the person who is afraid of taking risks. Perhaps this person will never be disappointed or disillusioned; perhaps she won't suffer the way people do when they have a dream to follow. But when that person looks back—and at some point everyone looks back—she will hear her heart saying, "What have you done with the miracles *that God planted in your days? What have you done with the talents God bestowed on you? You buried yourself in a cave because you were fearful of losing those talents. So this is your heritage: the certainty that you wasted your life."*

Pitiful are the people who must realize this. Because when they are finally able to believe in miracles, their life's magic moments will have already passed them by.

(9   (9   (9

AFTER THE LECTURE, members of the audience rushed up to him. I waited, worried about what his first impression of me would be after so many years. I felt like a child—insecure, tense because I knew none of his new friends, and jealous that he was paying more attention to the others than to me.

When he finally came up to me, he blushed. Suddenly he was no longer a man with important things to say but was once again the boy who had hidden with me at the hermitage of San Satúrio, telling me of his dream to travel the world (while our parents were calling the police, sure that we had drowned in the river).

"Pilar," he said.

I kissed him. I could have complimented him on his presentation. I could have said I was tired of being around so many people. I could have made some humorous remark about our childhood or commented on how proud I was to see him there, so admired by others.

I could have explained that I had to run and catch the last bus back to Zaragoza.

I could have. What does this phrase mean? At any given moment in our lives, there are certain things that could have happened but didn't. The magic moments go unrecognized, and then suddenly, the hand of destiny changes everything.

That's what happened to me just then. In spite of all the things I could have done or said, I asked a question that has brought me, a week later, to this river and has caused me to write these very lines.

"Can we have coffee together?" I said.

And he, turning to me, accepted the hand offered by fate.

"I really need to talk to you. Tomorrow I have a lecture in Bilbao. I have a car. Come with me."

"I have to get back to Zaragoza," I answered, not realizing that this was my last chance.

Then I surprised myself—perhaps because in seeing him, I had become a child again . . . or perhaps because we are not the ones who write the best moments of our lives. I said, "But they're about to celebrate the holiday of the Immaculate Conception in Bilbao. I can go there with you and then continue on to Zaragoza."

Just then, it was on the tip of my tongue to ask him about his being a "seminarian." He must have read my expression, because he said quickly, "Do you want to ask me something?"

"Yes. Before your lecture, a woman said that you were giving her back what had been hers. What did she mean?"

"Oh, that's nothing."

"But it's important to me. I don't know anything about your life; I'm even surprised to see so many people here."

He just laughed, and then he started to turn away to answer other people's questions.

"Wait," I said, grabbing his arm. "You didn't answer me."

"I don't think it would interest you, Pilar."

"I want to know anyway."

Taking a deep breath, he led me to a corner of the room. "All of the great religions—including Judaism, Catholicism, and Islam—are masculine. Men are in charge of the dogmas, men make the laws, and usually all the priests are men."

"Is that what the woman meant?"

He hesitated before he answered. "Yes. I have a different view of things: I believe in the feminine side of God."

I sighed with relief. The woman was mistaken; he couldn't be a seminarian because seminarians don't have such different views of things.

"You've explained it very well," I said.

(9   (9   (9

THE GIRL WHO HAD winked at me was waiting at the door.

"I know that we belong to the same tradition," she said. "My name is Brida."

"I don't know what you're talking about."

"Of course you do," she laughed.

She took my arm and led me out of the building before I could say anything more. It was a cold night, and I wasn't sure what I was going to do until we left for Bilbao the next morning.

"Where are we going?" I asked.

"To the statue of the Goddess."

"But . . . I need to find an inexpensive hotel where I can stay for the night."

"I'll show you one later."

I wanted to go to some warm café where I could talk to her for a bit and learn as much as I could about him. But I didn't want to argue. While she guided me across the Paseo de Castellana, I looked around at Madrid; I hadn't been there in years.

In the middle of the avenue, she stopped and pointed to the sky. "There She is."

The moon shone brilliantly through the bare branches of the trees on either side of the road.

"Isn't that beautiful!" I exclaimed.

But she wasn't listening. She spread her arms in the form of a cross, turning her palms upward, and just stood there contemplating the moon.

What have I gotten myself into? I thought. *I came here to attend a conference, and now I wind up in the Paseo de Castellana with this crazy girl. And tomorrow I'm going to Bilbao!*

"O mirror of the Earth Goddess," Brida was saying, her eyes closed. "Teach us about our power and make men understand us. Rising, gleaming, waning, and reviving in the heavens, you show us the cycle of the seed and the fruit."

She stretched her arms toward the night sky and held this position for some time. Several passersby looked at her and laughed, but she paid no attention; I was the one who was dying of embarrassment, standing there beside her.

"I needed to do that," she said, after her long adoration of the moon, "so that the Goddess would protect us."

"What are you talking about?"

"The same thing that your friend was talking about, only with words that are true."

I was sorry now that I hadn't paid closer attention to the lecture.

"We know the feminine side of God," Brida continued as we started to walk on. "We, the women, understand and love the Great Mother. We have paid for our wisdom with persecution and burnings at the stake, but we have survived. And now we understand Her mysteries."

Burnings at the stake? She was talking about witches!

I looked more closely at the woman by my side. She was pretty, with hair that hung to the middle of her back.

"While men were going off to hunt, we remained in the caves, in the womb of the Mother, caring for our children. And it was there that the Great Mother taught us everything.

"Men lived through movement, while we remained close to the womb of the Mother. This allowed us to see that seeds are turned into plants, and we told this to the men. We made the first bread, and we fed our people. We shaped the first cup so that we could drink. And we came to understand the cycle of creation, because our bodies repeat the rhythm of the moon."

She stopped suddenly. "There She is!"

I looked. There in the middle of the plaza, surrounded on all sides by traffic, was a fountain portraying a woman in a carriage drawn by lions.

"This is the Plaza Cybele," I said, trying to show off my knowledge of Madrid. I had seen this fountain on dozens of postcards.

But the young woman wasn't listening. She was already in the middle of the street, trying to make her way through the traffic. "Come on! Let's go over there!" she shouted, waving to me from the midst of the cars.

I decided to try to follow her, if only to get the name of a hotel. Her craziness was wearing me out; I needed to get some sleep.

We made it to the fountain at almost the same time; my heart was pounding, but she had a smile on her lips. "Water!" she exclaimed. "Water is Her manifestation."

"Please, I need the name of an inexpensive hotel."

She plunged her hands into the water. "You should do this, too," she said to me. "Feel the water."

"No! But I don't want to spoil your experience. I'm going to look for a hotel."

"Just a minute."

Brida took a small flute from her bag and began to play. To my surprise, the music had a hypnotic effect; the sounds of the traffic receded, and my racing heart began to slow down. I sat on the edge of the fountain, listening to the noise of the water and the sound of the flute, my eyes on the full moon gleaming above us. Somehow I was sensing—although I couldn't quite understand it—that the moon was a reflection of my womanhood.

I don't know how long she continued to play. When she stopped, she turned to the fountain. "Cybele, manifestation of the Great Mother, who governs the harvests, sustains the cities, and returns to woman her role as priestess . . ."

"Who are you?" I asked. "Why did you ask me to come with you?"

She turned to me. "I am what you see me to be. I am a part of the religion of the earth."

"What do you want from me?"

"I can read your eyes. I can read your heart. You are going to fall in love. And suffer."

"I am?"

"You know what I'm talking about. I saw how he was looking at you. He loves you."

This woman was really nuts!

"That's why I asked you to come with me—because he is important. Even though he says some silly things, at least he recognizes the Great Mother. Don't let him lose his way. Help him."

"You don't know what you're talking about. You're dreaming!" And I turned and rushed back into the traffic, swearing I'd forget everything she had said.

Sunday, December 5, 1993

❧ ❧ ❧

WE STOPPED for a cup of coffee.

"Yes, life teaches us many things," I said, trying to continue the conversation.

"It taught me that we can learn, and it taught me that we can change," he replied, "even when it seems impossible."

Clearly he wanted to drop the subject. We had hardly spoken during the two-hour drive that had brought us to this roadside café.

In the beginning, I had tried to reminisce about our childhood adventures, but he'd shown only a polite interest. In fact, he hadn't even really been listening to me; he kept asking me questions about things I had already told him.

Something was wrong. Had time and distance taken him away from my world forever? *After all, he talks about "magic moments," I reasoned. Why would he care about an old friend's career? He lives in a different universe, where Soria is only a remote memory—a town frozen in time, his childhood friends still young boys and girls, the old folks still alive and doing the same things they'd been doing for so many years.*

I was beginning to regret my decision to come with him. So when he changed the subject again, I resolved not to insist any further.

The last two hours of the drive to Bilbao were torture. He was watching the road, I was looking out the window, and neither of us could hide the bad feelings that had arisen between us. The rental car didn't have a radio, so all we could do was endure the silence.

"Let's ask where the bus station is," I suggested as soon as we left the highway. "The buses leave from here regularly for Zaragoza."

It was the hour of siesta, and there were few people in the streets. We passed one gentleman and then a couple of teenagers, but he didn't stop to ask them. "Do you know where it is?" I spoke up, after some time had passed.

"Where what is?"

He still wasn't paying attention to what I said.

And then suddenly I understood what the silence was about. What did he have in common with a woman who had never ventured out into the world? How could he possibly be interested in spending time with someone who feared the unknown, who preferred a secure job and a conventional marriage to the life he led? Poor me, chattering away about friends from childhood and dusty memories of an insignificant village—those were the only things I could discuss.

When we seemed to have reached the center of town, I said, "You can let me off here." I was trying to sound casual, but I felt stupid, childish, and irritated.

He didn't stop the car.

"I have to catch the bus back to Zaragoza," I insisted.

"I've never been here before," he answered. "I have no idea where my hotel is, I don't know where the conference is being held, and I don't know where the bus station is."

"Don't worry, I'll be all right."

He slowed down but kept on driving.

"I'd really like to . . . ," he began. He tried again but still couldn't finish his thought.

I could imagine what he would like to do: thank me for the company, send greetings to his old friends—maybe that would break the tension.

"I would really like it if you went with me to the conference tonight," he finally said.

I was shocked. Was he stalling for time so that he could make up for the awkward silence of our trip?

"I'd really like you to go with me," he repeated.

Now, maybe I'm a girl from the farm with no great stories to tell. Maybe I lack the sophistication of women from the big city. Life in the country may not make a woman elegant or worldly, but it still teaches her how to listen to her heart and to trust her instincts.

To my surprise, my instincts told me that he meant what he said.

I sighed with relief. Of course I wasn't going to stay for any conference, but at least my friend seemed to be back. He was even inviting me along on his adventures, wanting to share his fears and triumphs with me.

"Thanks for the invitation," I said, "but I don't have enough money for a hotel, and I do need to get back to my studies."

"I have some money. You can stay in my room. We'll ask for two beds."

I noticed that he was beginning to perspire, despite

the chill in the air. My heart sounded an alarm, and all the joy of the moment before turned into confusion.

Suddenly he stopped the car and looked directly into my eyes.

No one can lie, no one can hide anything, when he looks directly into someone's eyes. And any woman with the least bit of sensitivity can read the eyes of a man in love.

I thought immediately of what that weird young woman at the fountain had said. It wasn't possible—but it seemed to be true.

I had never dreamed that after all these years he would still remember. When we were children, we had walked through the world hand in hand. I had loved him—if a child can know what love means. But that was so many years ago—it was another life, a life whose innocence had opened my heart to all that was good.

And now we were responsible adults. We had put away childish things.

I looked into his eyes. I didn't want to—or wasn't able to—believe what I saw there.

"I just have this last conference, and then the holidays of the Immaculate Conception begin. I have to go up into the mountains; I want to show you something."

This brilliant man who was able to speak of magic moments was now here with me, acting as awkward as could be. He was moving too fast, he was unsure of himself; the things he was proposing were confused. It was painful for me to see him this way.

I opened the door and got out, then leaned against the fender, looking at the nearly deserted street. I lit a cigarette. I could try to hide my thoughts, pretend that I didn't understand what he was saying; I could try to convince myself that this was just a suggestion made by one childhood friend to another. Maybe he'd been on the road too long and was beginning to get confused.

Maybe I was exaggerating.

He jumped out of the car and came to my side.

"I'd really like you to stay for the conference tonight," he said again. "But if you can't, I'll understand."

There! The world made a complete turn and returned to where it belonged. It wasn't what I had been thinking; he was no longer insisting, he was ready to let me leave—a man in love doesn't act that way.

I felt both stupid and relieved. Yes, I could stay for at least one more day. We could have dinner together and get a little drunk—something we'd never done when we were younger. This would give me a chance to forget the stupid ideas I'd just had, and it would be a good opportunity to break the ice that had frozen us ever since we left Madrid.

One day wouldn't make any difference. And then at least I'd have a story to tell my friends.

"Separate beds," I said, joking. "And you pay for dinner, because I'm still a student. I'm broke."

We put our bags in the hotel room and came down to see where the conference was to be held. Since we were so early, we sat down in a café to wait.

"I want to give you something," he said, handing me a small red pouch.

I opened it and found inside an old rusty medal, with Our Lady of Grace on one side and the Sacred Heart of Jesus on the other.

"That was yours," he said, noticing my surprise. My heart began to sound the alarm again. "One day—it was autumn, just like it is now, and we must have been ten—I was sitting with you in the plaza where the great oak stood.

"I was going to tell you something, something I had rehearsed for weeks. But as soon as I began, you told me that you had lost your medal at the hermitage of San Satúrio, and you asked me to see if I could find it there."

I remembered. Oh, God, I remembered!

"I did find it. But when I returned to the plaza, I no longer had the courage to say what I had rehearsed. So I promised myself that I would return the medal to you only when I was able to complete the sentence that I'd begun that day almost twenty years ago. For a long time, I've tried to forget it, but it's always there. I can't live with it any longer."

He put down his coffee, lit a cigarette, and looked at the ceiling for a long time. Then he turned to me. "It's a very simple sentence," he said. "I love you."

*SOMETIMES AN UNCONTROLLABLE feeling of sad-
ness grips us*, he said. *We recognize that the magic moment of the
day has passed and that we've done nothing about it. Life begins to
conceal its magic and its art.*

*We have to listen to the child we once were, the child who still ex-
ists inside us. That child understands magic moments. We can stifle its
cries, but we cannot silence its voice.*

*The child we once were is still there. Blessed are the children, for
theirs is the kingdom of heaven.*

*If we are not reborn——if we cannot learn to look at life with the
innocence and the enthusiasm of childhood——it makes no sense to go
on living.*

*There are many ways to commit suicide. Those who try to kill
the body violate God's law. Those who try to kill the soul also violate
God's law, even though their crime is less visible to others.*

*We have to pay attention to what the child in our heart tells us.
We should not be embarrassed by this child. We must not allow
this child to be scared because the child is alone and is almost never
heard.*

*We must allow the child to take the reins of our lives. The child
knows that each day is different from every other day.*

*We have to allow it to feel loved again. We must please this
child——even if this means that we act in ways we are not used to,
in ways that may seem foolish to others.*

Remember that human wisdom is madness in the eyes of God. But if we listen to the child who lives in our soul, our eyes will grow bright. If we do not lose contact with that child, we will not lose contact with life.

ဖ ဖ ဖ

THE COLORS AROUND ME were growing vivid; I felt that I was speaking with more intensity and that my glass made a louder sound when I put it down on the table.

A group of about ten of us were having dinner together after the conference. Everyone was speaking at the same time, and I was smiling, for this night was special: it was the first night in many years that I had not planned.

What a joy!

When I'd decided to go to Madrid, I had been in control of my actions and my feelings. Now, suddenly, all that had changed. Here I was in a city where I'd never set foot before, even though it was only three hours from the place where I'd been born. I was sitting at a table where I knew only one person, and everyone was speaking to me as if they'd known me for years. I was amazed that I could enter into the conversation, that I could drink and enjoy myself with them.

I was there because suddenly life had presented me with Life. I felt no guilt, no fear, no embarrassment. As I listened to what he was saying—and felt myself growing closer to him—I was more and more convinced that he was right: there are moments when you have to take a risk, to do crazy things.

I spend day after day with my texts and notebooks, making this superhuman effort just to purchase my own servitude, I thought. *Why do I want that job? What does it offer me as a human being, as a woman?*

Nothing! I wasn't born to spend my life behind a desk, helping judges dispose of their cases.

No, I can't think that way about my life. I'm going to have to return to it this week. It must be the wine. After all, when all is said and done, if you don't work, you don't eat. This is all a dream. It's going to end.

But how long can I make the dream go on?

For the first time I considered going to the mountains with him for the next few days. After all, a week of holidays was about to begin.

"Who are you?" a woman at our table asked me.

"A childhood friend," I answered.

"Was he doing these things when he was a child, too?"

"What things?"

The conversation at the table seemed to fade and then die out.

"You know: the miracles."

"He could always speak well." I didn't understand what she meant.

Everyone laughed, including him. I had no idea what was going on. But—maybe because of the wine—I felt relaxed, and for once I didn't feel like I had to be in control.

I looked around and then said something that I forgot the next moment. I was thinking about the upcoming holiday.

It was good to be here, meeting new people, talking about serious things but always with a touch of humor. I felt like I was really participating in the world. For at least this one night, I was no longer just seeing the real world through television or the newspapers. When I returned to Zaragoza, I'd have stories to tell. If I accepted his invitation for the holidays, I'd have whole years of memories to live on.

He was so right not to pay any attention to my remarks about Soria, I thought. And I began to feel sorry for myself; for so many years, my drawer full of memories had held the same old stories.

"Have some more wine," a white-haired man said, filling my glass.

I drank it down. I kept thinking about how few things I would have had to tell my children and grandchildren if I hadn't come with him.

"I'm counting on our trip to France," he said to me so that only I could hear.

The wine had freed my tongue. "But only if you understand one thing."

"What's that?"

"It's about what you said before the conference. At the café."

"The medal?"

"No," I said, looking into his eyes and doing everything I could to appear sober. "What you said."

"We'll talk about it later," he said, quickly trying to change the subject.

He had said that he loved me. We hadn't had time to talk about it, but I knew I could convince him that it wasn't true.

"If you want me to take the trip with you, you have to listen to me," I said.

"I don't want to talk about it here. We're having a good time."

"You left Soria when you were very young," I went on. "I'm only a link to your past. I've reminded you of your roots, and that's what makes you think as you do. But that's all it is. There can't be any love involved."

He listened but didn't answer. Someone asked him his opinion about something, and our conversation was interrupted.

At least I've explained how I feel, I thought. *The love he was talking about only exists in fairy tales.*

In real life, love has to be possible. Even if it is not returned right away, love can only survive when the hope exists that you will be able to win over the person you desire.

Anything else is fantasy.

From the other side of the table, as if he had guessed what I was thinking, he raised his glass in a toast. "To love," he said.

I could tell that he, too, was a little drunk. So I decided to take advantage of the opening: "To those wise enough to understand that sometimes love is nothing more than the foolishness of childhood," I said.

"The wise are wise only because they love. And the foolish are foolish only because they think they can understand love," he answered.

The others at the table heard him, and in a moment an animated discussion about love was in full swing. Everyone had a strong opinion and was defending their position tooth and nail; it took more wine to calm things down. Finally someone said it was getting late and that the owner of the restaurant wanted to close.

"We have five days of vacation," someone shouted from another table. "If the owner wants to close, it's just because you were getting too serious."

Everyone laughed—except me.

"Then where can we talk about serious things?" someone asked the drunk at the other table.

"In church!" said the drunk. And this time all of us laughed.

My friend stood up. I thought he was going to start a fight, because we were all acting like adolescents, and that's what adolescents do. Fighting is as much a part of being a teenager as the kisses, the secret embraces, the loud music, and the fast pace.

But instead he took my hand and moved toward the door. "We should go," he said. "It's getting late."

(9   (9   (9

IT WAS RAINING in Bilbao.

Lovers need to know how to lose themselves and then how to find themselves again. He was able to do both well. Now he was happy, and as we returned to the hotel he sang:

Son los locos que inventaron el amor.

The song was right: it must have been the lunatics who invented love.

I was still feeling the effects of the wine, but I was struggling to think clearly. I had to stay in control of the situation if I wanted to make the trip with him.

But it will be easy to be in control because I'm not too emotional, I thought. *Anyone who can conquer her heart can conquer the world.*

Con un poema y un trombón
a develarte el corazón

To lose my heart to you with a poem and a trombone. I wish I didn't have to control my heart. If I could surrender, even if only for a weekend, this rain falling on my face would feel different. If love were easy, I would be embracing him now, and the words of his song would be our story. If Zaragoza weren't waiting for me after the holidays, I'd want to stay drunk and be free to kiss him, caress him, say the things and hear the things that lovers say and do to each other.

But no! I can't. I don't want to.

Salgamos a volar, querida mia, the song says.

Yes, let's fly away. But under my conditions.

He still didn't know that I was going to say yes to his invitation. Why did I want to take this risk?

Because I was drunk, because I was tired of days that were all the same.

But this weariness will pass. I'm going to want to get back to Zaragoza, where I have chosen to live. My studies are waiting for me. The husband I'm still looking for is waiting for me—a husband who won't be as difficult to find.

An easier life waits for me, with children and grandchildren, with a clear budget and a yearly vacation. I don't know what his fears are, but I know my own. I don't need new fears—my own are enough.

I was sure I could never fall in love with someone like him. I knew him too well, all his weaknesses and fears. I just couldn't admire him as the others seemed to.

But love is much like a dam: if you allow a tiny crack to form through which only a trickle of water can pass, that trickle will quickly bring down the whole structure, and soon no one will be able to control the force of the current.

For when those walls come down, then love takes over, and it no longer matters what is possible or impossible; it doesn't even matter whether we can keep the loved one at our side. To love is to lose control.

No, no, I cannot allow such a crack to form. No matter how small.

"Hey, hold up a minute!"

He stopped singing immediately. Quick steps echoed on the damp pavement behind us.

"Let's get out of here," he said, grabbing my arm.

"Wait!" a man shouted. "I need to talk to you!"

But he moved ahead even more rapidly. "This has nothing to do with us," he said. "Let's get to the hotel."

Yet it did have to do with us—there was no one else on the street. My heart was beating fast, and the effects of the wine disappeared altogether. I remembered that Bilbao was in Basque country and that terrorist attacks were common. The man's footsteps came closer.

"Let's go," he said, hurrying along.

But it was too late. A man's figure, soaked from head to foot, stepped in front of us.

"Stop, please!" the man said. "For the love of God."

I was frightened. I looked around frantically for a means of escape, hoping that by some miracle a police car would appear. Instinctively, I clutched at his arm—but he pulled away.

"Please!" said the man. "I heard that you were in the city. I need your help. It's my son." The man knelt on the pavement and began to weep. "Please," he said, "please!"

My friend gasped for breath; I watched as he lowered his head and closed his eyes. For a few minutes the silence was broken only by the sound of the rain and the sobs of the man kneeling on the sidewalk.

"Go to the hotel, Pilar," he said finally. "Get some sleep. I won't be back until dawn."

Monday, December 6, 1993

❧   ❧   ❧

LOVE IS A TRAP. When it appears, we see only its light, not its shadows.

"Look at the land around here!" he said. "Let's lie down on the ground and feel the planet's heart beating!"

"But I'll get my coat dirty, and it's the only one I have with me."

We were driving through hills of olive groves. After yesterday's rain in Bilbao, the morning sun made me sleepy. I hadn't brought sunglasses—I hadn't brought anything, since I'd expected to return to Zaragoza two days ago. I'd had to sleep in a shirt he loaned me, and I'd bought a T-shirt at a shop near the hotel in Bilbao so that at least I could wash the one I was wearing.

"You must be sick of seeing me in the same clothes every day," I said, trying to make a joke about something trivial to see if that would make all this seem real.

"I'm glad you're here."

He hadn't mentioned love again since he had given me the medal, but he had been in a good mood; he seemed to be eighteen again. Now he walked along beside me bathed in the clear morning light.

"What do you have to do over there?" I asked, pointing toward the peaks of the Pyrenees on the horizon.

"Beyond those mountains lies France," he answered with a smile.

"I know—I studied geography, too, you know. I'm just curious about why we have to go there."

He paused, smiling to himself. "So you can take a look at a house you might be interested in."

"If you're thinking about becoming a real estate agent, forget it. I don't have any money."

It didn't matter to me whether we visited a village in Navarra or went all the way to France. I just didn't want to spend the holidays in Zaragoza.

You see? I heard my brain say to my heart. *You're happy that you've accepted his invitation. You've changed—you just haven't recognized it yet.*

No, I hadn't changed at all. I was just relaxing a little.

"Look at the stones on the ground."

They were rounded, with no sharp edges. They looked like pebbles from the sea. But the sea had never been here in the fields of Navarra.

"The feet of laborers, pilgrims, and explorers smoothed these stones," he said. "The stones were changed—and the travelers were too."

"Has traveling taught you all the things you know?"

"No. I learned from the miracles of revelation."

I didn't understand, but I didn't pursue it. For now, I was content to bask in the beauty of the sun, the fields, and the mountains.

"Where are we going now?" I asked.

"Nowhere. Let's just enjoy the morning, the sun, and the countryside. We have a long trip ahead of us." He hesitated for a moment and then asked, "Do you still have the medal?"

"Sure, I've kept it," I said, and began to walk faster. I didn't want to talk about the medal—I didn't want to talk about anything that might ruin the happiness and freedom of our morning together.

❧ ❧ ❧

A VILLAGE APPEARED. Like most medieval cities, it was situated atop a mountain peak; even from a distance, I could see the tower of a church and the ruins of a castle.

"Let's drive to that village," I suggested.

Although he seemed reluctant, he agreed. I could see a chapel along the road, and I wanted to stop and go in. I didn't pray anymore, but the silence of churches always attracted me.

Don't feel guilty, I was saying to myself. *If he's in love, that's his problem.* He had asked about the medal. I knew that he was hoping we'd get back to our conversation at the café. But I was afraid of hearing something I didn't want to hear. *I won't get into it, I won't bring up the subject.*

But what if he really did love me? What if he thought that we could transform this love into something deeper?

Ridiculous, I thought to myself. *There's nothing deeper than love. In fairy tales, the princesses kiss the frogs, and the frogs become princes. In real life, the princesses kiss princes, and the princes turn into frogs.*

After driving for another half hour, we reached the chapel. An old man was seated on the steps. He was the first person we'd seen since our drive began.

It was the end of fall, and, in keeping with tradition, the fields had been returned once more to the Lord, who would fertilize the land with his blessings and allow human beings to harvest his sustenance by the sweat of their brows.

"Hello," he said to the man.

"How are you?"

"What is the name of this village?"

"San Martín de Unx."

"Unx?" I said. "It sounds like the name of a gnome."

The old man didn't understand the joke. Disappointed, I walked toward the entrance to the chapel.

"You can't go in," warned the old man. "It closed at noon. If you like, you can come back at four this afternoon."

The door was open and I could look inside, although it was so bright out that I couldn't see clearly.

"Just for a minute?" I asked. "I'd like to say a prayer."

"I'm very sorry. It's already closed."

He was listening to my conversation with the old man but didn't say anything.

"All right, then, let's leave," I said. "There's no point in arguing."

He continued to look at me, his gaze empty, distant. "Don't you want to see the chapel?" he asked.

I could see he didn't approve of my decision. *He thinks I'm weak, cowardly, unable to fight for what I want. Even without a kiss, the princess is transformed into a frog.*

"Remember yesterday?" I said. "You ended our conversation in the bar because you didn't want to argue with me. Now when I do the same thing, you criticize me."

The old man watched our discussion impassively. He was probably happy that something was actually happening, there in a place where all the mornings, all the afternoons, and all the nights were the same.

"The door to the church is open," he said, speaking to the old man. "If you want some money, we can give you some. But she wants to see the church."

"It's too late."

"Fine. We'll go in anyway." He took my arm and we went in.

My heart was pounding. The old man could get nasty, call the police, ruin the trip.

"Why are you doing this?"

"Because you wanted to see the chapel."

I was so nervous I couldn't even focus on what was inside. The argument—and my attitude—had ruined our perfect morning.

I listened carefully for any sounds from outside. *The old man might call the village police,* I thought. *Trespassers in the chapel! Thieves! They're breaking the law!* The old man had said the chapel was closed, that visiting hours were over. *He's a poor old man, unable to keep us from going in. And the police will be tough on us because we offended a feeble old man.*

I stayed inside the chapel just long enough to show that I'd really wanted to see it. As soon as enough time had passed for an imaginary Ave Maria, I said, "Let's go."

"Don't be frightened, Pilar. Don't just fall into playing a role."

I didn't want my problem with the old man to become a problem with him, so I tried to stay calm. "I don't know what you mean by 'playing a role.'"

"Some people always have to be doing battle with someone, sometimes even with themselves, battling with their own lives. So they begin to create a kind of play in their head, and they write the script based on their frustrations."

"I know a lot of people like that. I know just what you mean."

"But the worst part is that they cannot present the play by themselves," he continued. "So they begin to invite other actors to join in.

"That's what that fellow outside was doing. He wanted revenge for something, and he chose us to play a part. If we had accepted his restrictions, we'd be regretting it now. We would have been defeated. We would have agreed to participate in his miserable life and in his frustrations.

"The man's aggression was easy to see, so it was easy for us to refuse the role he wanted us to play. But other people also 'invite' us to behave like victims, when they complain about the unfairness of life, for example, and ask us to agree, to offer advice, to participate."

He looked into my eyes. "Be careful. When you join in that game, you always wind up losing."

He was right. But I still wasn't happy about being inside the chapel. "OK, but I've already said my prayer. I've done what I wanted to do. Let's go."

The contrast between the darkness inside the chapel and the strong sunlight blinded me for a few moments. When my eyes adjusted, I saw that the old man was no longer there.

"Let's have some lunch," he said, walking in the direction of the village.

۶   ۶   ۶

I DRANK TWO GLASSES of wine at lunch. I'd never done that in my life.

He was speaking to the waiter, who told him that there were several Roman ruins in the area. I was trying to listen to their conversation, but I was having trouble stifling my bad mood.

The princess had turned into a frog. So what? Who do I have to prove anything to? I wasn't looking for anything—not for a man and certainly not for love.

I knew it, I said to myself. *I knew he was going to turn my world upside down. My brain warned me, but my heart didn't want to take its advice.*

I've paid a considerable price for the little I have gained. I've been forced to deny myself many things I've wanted, to abandon so many roads that were open to me. I've sacrificed my dreams in the name of a larger dream—a peaceful soul. I didn't want to give up that peace.

"You're tense," he said, breaking off his conversation with the waiter.

"Yes, I am. I think that old man went for the police. I think this is a small place, and they know where we are. I think this boldness of yours about having lunch here could wind up ruining our holiday."

He twirled his glass of water. Surely he knew that this was not the problem—that I was actually ashamed.

Why do we always do this? Why do we notice the speck in our eye but not the mountains, the fields, the olive groves?

"Listen, that's not going to happen," he said. "The old man has gone home and has already forgotten the whole thing. Trust me."

That's not why I'm so tense, you idiot.

"Listen to your heart more," he went on.

"That's just it! I *am* listening to it," I said. "And I feel that we should leave. I'm not enjoying this place."

"You shouldn't drink during the day. It doesn't help anything."

Up to that point, I'd controlled myself. Now it was time to say what I thought.

"You think you know everything," I said, "that you know all about magic moments, the inner child . . . I don't know what you're doing here with me."

He laughed. "I admire you. And I admire the battle you're waging with your heart."

"What battle?"

"Never mind," he said.

But I knew what he was talking about.

"Don't kid yourself," I said. "We can talk about it if you like. You're mistaken about my feelings."

He stopped fooling with his glass and looked at me. "No, I'm not mistaken. I know you don't love me."

This confused me even more.

"But I'm going to fight for your love," he continued. "There are some things in life that are worth fighting for to the end."

I was speechless.

"You are worth it," he said.

I turned away, trying to pretend that I was interested in the restaurant's decor. I had been feeling like a frog, and suddenly I was a princess again.

I want to believe what you're saying, I thought to myself. *It won't change anything, but at least I won't feel so weak, so in-capable.*

"I apologize for my outburst," I said.

He smiled, signaled to the waiter, and paid the check.

On the way back to the car, I became confused again. Maybe it was the sun—but no, it was autumn, and the sun was weak. Perhaps the old man—but he disappeared a while ago.

All this was so new to me. Life takes us by surprise and orders us to move toward the unknown—even when we don't want to and when we think we don't need to.

I tried to concentrate on the scenery, but I couldn't focus on the olive groves, the village atop the mountain, the chapel with the old man at the gate. All of it was so unfamiliar.

I remembered how much I'd drunk the day before and the song he had sung:

Las tardecitas de Buenos Aires tienen este no sé . . .
¿Qué sé yo?
Viste, salí de tu casa, por Arenales . . .

Why sing of the nights of Buenos Aires, when we were in Bilbao? I didn't live on a street called Arenales. What had gotten into him?

"What was that song you were singing yesterday?" I asked.

"*Balada para un loco,*" he said. "Why do you ask about it now?"

"I don't know."

But I had a reason: I knew he'd sung the song as a kind of snare. He'd made me memorize the words, just as I would memorize course work for an examination. He could have sung a song I was familiar with—but he'd chosen one I'd never heard before.

It was a trap. Later, if I heard the song played on the radio or at a club, I'd think of him, of Bilbao, and of a time in my life when autumn turned to spring. I'd recall the excitement, the adventure, and the child who was reborn out of God knows where.

That's what he was thinking. He was wise, experienced; he knew how to woo the woman he wanted.

I'm going crazy, I told myself. *I must be an alcoholic, drinking so much two days in a row. He knows all the tricks. He's controlling me, leading me along with his sweetness.*

"I admire the battle you are waging with your heart," he had said at the restaurant.

But he was wrong. Because I had fought with my heart and defeated it long ago. I was certainly not going to become passionate about something that was impossible. I knew my limits; I knew how much suffering I could bear.

"Say something," I demanded, as we walked back to the car.

"What?"

"Anything. Talk to me."

So he began to tell me about the visions of the Virgin Mary at Fátima. I don't know why he came up with that, but the story of the three shepherds who had spoken to the Virgin distracted me.

My heart relaxed. *Yes, I know my limits, and I know how to stay in control.*

۶ ۶ ۶

WE ARRIVED AT NIGHT in a fog so dense we could hardly see where we were. I could make out only a small plaza, a lamppost, some medieval houses barely illuminated by the yellow light, and a well.

"The fog!" he exclaimed.

I couldn't understand why he was so excited.

"We're in Saint-Savin," he explained.

The name meant nothing to me. But we were in France, and that in itself thrilled me.

"Why this place?" I asked.

"Because the house I want you to see is here," he answered, laughing. "Also, I promised that I would come back here on the day of the Immaculate Conception."

"Here?"

"Well, near here."

He stopped the car. When we stepped out, he took my hand, and we began to walk through the fog.

"This place became a part of my life quite unexpectedly," he said.

You too? I thought.

"When I first came here, I thought I was lost. But I wasn't—actually, I was just rediscovering it."

"You talk in riddles sometimes," I said.

"This is where I realized how much I needed you in my life."

I looked away; I couldn't understand him. "But what does that have to do with losing your way?"

"Let's find someone who'll rent us a room, because the two hotels in this village are only open during the summer. Then we'll have dinner at a good restaurant—no tension, no fear of the police, no need to think about running back to the car! And when the wine loosens our tongues, we'll talk about many things."

We both laughed. I already felt more relaxed. During the drive here, I had looked back over the wild things I'd been thinking. And as we crossed over the top of the mountains that separate France from Spain, I'd asked God to cleanse my soul of tension and fear.

I was tired of playing the child and acting the way many of my friends did—the ones who are afraid that love is impossible without even knowing what love is. If I stayed like that, I would miss out on everything good that these few days with him might offer.

Careful, I thought. *Watch out for the break in the dam. If that break occurs, nothing in the world will be able to stop it.*

"May the Virgin protect us from here on," he said.

I remained silent.

"Why didn't you say 'amen'?" he asked.

"Because I don't think that's important anymore. There was a time when religion was a part of my life, but that time has passed."

He turned around and began to walk back to the car. "I still pray," I went on. "I prayed as we were crossing the Pyrenees. But it's something automatic, and I'm not even sure I still believe in it."

"Why?"

"Because I've suffered, and God didn't listen to my prayers. Because many times in my life I have tried to love with all my heart, and my love has wound up being trampled or betrayed. If God is love, he should have cared more about my feelings.

"God *is* love. But the one who understands this best is the Virgin."

I burst out laughing. When I turned to look at him, I saw that he was serious—this was not a joke.

"The Virgin understands the mystery of total surrender," he went on. "And having loved and suffered, she freed us from pain. In the same way that Jesus freed us from sin."

"Jesus was the son of God. They say that the Virgin was merely a woman who happened to receive him into her womb," I said. I was trying to make up for my laughter and let him know that I respected his faith.

He opened the car door and took out our bags. When I tried to take mine from his hand, he smiled.

"Let me carry your bag."

No one's done that for me in a long time, I thought.

We knocked on the door of the first house, but the woman said she didn't rent rooms. At the second door, no one answered. At the third, a kind old man greeted us—but when we looked at the room, there was only a double bed. I turned it down.

"Maybe we should head for a larger city," I suggested as we left.

"We'll find a room," he said. "Do you know the exercise of the Other? It's part of a story written a hundred years ago, whose author . . . "

"Forget the author, and tell me the story," I interrupted. We were once more walking along the only street in Saint-Savin.

(; (; (;

A MAN RUNS INTO an old friend who had somehow never been able to make it in life. "I should give him some money," he thinks. But instead he learns that his old friend has grown rich and is actually seeking him out to repay the debts he had run up over the years.

They go to a bar they used to frequent together, and the friend buys drinks for everyone there. When they ask him how he became so successful, he answers that until only a few days ago, he had been living the role of the "Other."

"What is the Other?" they ask.

"The Other is the one who taught me what I should be like, but not what I am. The Other believes that it is our obligation to spend our entire life thinking about how to get our hands on as much money as possible so that we will not die of hunger when we are old. So we think so much about money and our plans for acquiring it that we discover we are alive only when our days on earth are practically done. And then it's too late."

"And you? Who are you?"

"I am just like everyone else who listens to their heart: a person who is enchanted by the mystery of life. Who is open to miracles, who experiences joy and enthusiasm for what they do. It's just that the Other, afraid of disappointment, kept me from taking action."

"But there is suffering in life," one of the listeners said.

"And there are defeats. No one can avoid them. But it's better to lose some of the battles in the struggle for your dreams than to be defeated without ever even knowing what you're fighting for."

"That's it?" another listener asked.

"Yes, that's it. When I learned this, I resolved to become the person I had always wanted to be. The Other stood there in the corner of my room, watching me, but I will never let the Other into myself again—even though it has already tried to frighten me, warning me that it's risky not to think about the future.

"From the moment that I ousted the Other from my life, the Divine Energy began to perform its miracles."

❧   ❧   ❧

IN SPITE OF the fact that my friend had long ago expelled the Other from his life, he still wasn't having much luck finding us lodging for the night. But I knew he hadn't told me that story for his own sake—he had told it for mine. He seemed to be talking about my fears, my insecurity, and my unwillingness to see what was wonderful because tomorrow it might disappear and then I would suffer.

The gods throw the dice, and they don't ask whether we want to be in the game or not. They don't care if when you go, you leave behind a lover, a home, a career, or a dream. The gods don't care whether you have it all, whether it seems that your every desire can be met through hard work and persistence. The gods don't want to know about your plans and your hopes. Somewhere they're throwing the dice—and you are chosen. From then on, winning or losing is only a question of luck.

The gods throw the dice, freeing love from its cage. And love can create or destroy—depending on the direction of the wind when it is set free.

For the moment, the wind was blowing in his favor. But the wind is as capricious as the gods—and deep inside myself, I had begun to feel some gusts.

ϛ ϛ ϛ

AT LAST, as if fate wanted to show me that the story of the Other was true—and the universe always conspires to help the dreamer—we found a house to stay in, with a room with separate beds. My first move was to bathe, wash my clothes, and put on the shirt I had bought. I felt refreshed, and this made me feel more secure.

After having dinner with the couple who owned the house—the restaurants were also closed during the autumn and winter—he asked for a bottle of wine, promising to replace it the next day. We put on our coats, borrowed two glasses, and went out.

"Let's sit on the edge of the well," I suggested.

And there we sat, drinking to keep the cold and the tension away.

"It looks like the Other has gotten to you," I joked. "Your good mood seems to have disappeared."

He laughed. "I knew we were going to find a room, and we did. The universe always helps us fight for our dreams, no matter how foolish they may be. Our dreams are our own, and only we can know the effort required to keep them alive."

In the fog, which hung yellow under the glow of the street lamp, we couldn't see even as far as the other side of the plaza.

I took a deep breath. We couldn't avoid the subject any longer.

"We have to talk about love," I said. "You know how I've been these last few days. If it had been up to me, the subject would never have come up. But ever since you brought it up, I haven't been able to stop thinking about it."

"It's risky, falling in love."

"I know that," I answered. "I've been in love before. It's like a narcotic. At first it brings the euphoria of complete surrender. The next day, you want more. You're not addicted yet, but you like the sensation, and you think you can still control things. You think about the person you love for two minutes, and forget them for three hours.

"But then you get used to that person, and you begin to be completely dependent on them. Now you think about him for three hours and forget him for two minutes. If he's not there, you feel like an addict who can't get a fix. And just as addicts steal and humiliate themselves to get what they need, you're willing to do anything for love."

"What a horrible way to put it," he said.

It really was a horrible way to put it; my analogy didn't go with the romance of the evening—the wine, the well, and the medieval houses in the plaza. But it was true. If he was going to base so many of his actions on love, he needed to know what the risks were.

"So we should love only those who can stay near us," I said.

He looked out at the fog. Now he no longer seemed interested in whether we negotiated the dangerous waters of a conversation about love. I was being tough, but there was no other way.

Subject closed, I thought. *Our being together for these three days has been enough to change his mind.* My pride was a bit wounded, but my heart was relieved. *Do I really want this?* I asked myself. I realized that I was already beginning to sense the storms brought on by the winds of love. I had already begun to feel the break in the dam.

We drank for some time without bringing up anything serious. We talked about the couple who owned the house and the saint for whom the town had been named. He told me some of the legends about the church across the square, which I could barely see in the fog.

"You're upset," he said at one point.

Yes, my mind was wandering. I wished I were there with someone who could bring peace to my heart—someone with whom I could spend a little time without being afraid that I would lose him the next day. With that reassurance, the time would pass more slowly. We could be silent for a while because we'd know we had the rest of our lives together for conversation. I wouldn't have to worry about serious matters, about difficult decisions and hard words.

❧ ❧ ❧

W E SAT THERE in silence—and that in itself was a sign. For the first time, we had nothing to say, although I only noticed this when he stood up to go find us another bottle of wine.

Silence. Then I heard the sound of his footsteps returning to the well where we'd been sitting for more than an hour, drinking and staring at the fog.

This was the first time we'd been silent for so long. It was not the awkward silence of the trip from Madrid to Bilbao. And not the silence of my fearful heart when we were in the chapel near San Martín de Unx.

This was a silence that spoke for itself. A silence that said we no longer needed to explain things to each other.

The sound of his footsteps halted. He was looking at me—and what he saw must have been beautiful: a woman seated on the edge of a well, on a foggy night, in the light of the street lamp.

The ancient houses, the eleventh-century church, and the silence.

The second bottle of wine was half empty when I decided to speak.

"This morning, I convinced myself that I was an alcoholic. I've been drinking from morning to night. In these past three days, I've drunk more than in the entire past year."

He reached out and stroked my hair without saying anything. I absorbed his touch without trying to pull away.

"Tell me about your life since I last saw you," I asked.

"There are no great mysteries to tell. My path is always there, and I do everything I can to follow it in a dignified way."

"What is your path?"

"The path of someone seeking love."

He hesitated for a moment, fiddling with the near-empty bottle.

"And love's path is really complicated," he concluded.

"Because on that path we can go either to heaven or to hell?" I wasn't sure whether he was referring to us or not.

He didn't respond. Perhaps he was still deep in the ocean of silence, but the wine had loosened my tongue again, and I had to speak.

"You said that something here in this city altered your course."

"Yes, I think it did. I'm still not absolutely sure, and that's why I wanted to bring you here."

"Is this some kind of test?"

"No. It's a surrender. So that She will help me to make the right decision."

"Who will?"

"The Virgin."

The Virgin! I should have known. I was surprised that all his years of travel, of learning, of new horizons hadn't freed him from the Catholicism of his childhood. In at least this respect, my friends and I had come a long way—we no longer lived under the weight of guilt and sin.

"I'm surprised that after all you've been through, you still keep the faith."

"I haven't kept it. I lost it and recovered it."

"But a faith in virgins? In impossible things and in fantasies? Haven't you had an active sex life?"

"Well, normal. I've been in love with many women."

To my surprise, I felt a stab of jealousy. But my inner battle seemed already to have subsided, and I didn't want to start it up again.

"Why is she 'The Virgin'? Why isn't She presented to us as a normal woman, like any other?"

He drained the few drops remaining in the bottle and asked if I wanted him to go for another. I said no.

"What I want is an answer from you. Every time we start to speak about certain things, you try to talk about something else."

"She *was* normal. She had already had other children. The Bible tells us that Jesus had two brothers. Virginity, as it relates to Jesus, is based on a different thing: Mary initiated a new generation of grace. A new era began. She is the cosmic bride, Earth, which opens to the heavens and allows itself to be fertilized.

"Because of the courage She showed in accepting her destiny, She allowed God to come down to earth—and She was transformed into the Great Mother."

I didn't understand exactly what he was telling me, and he could see that.

"She is the feminine face of God. She has her own divinity."

He spoke with great emotion; in fact, his words almost sounded forced, as if he felt he was committing a sin.

"A goddess?" I asked.

I waited for him to explain, but he couldn't say anything more. I thought about his Catholicism and about how what he had just said seemed blasphemous.

"Who is the Virgin? What is the Goddess?"

"It's not easy to explain," he said, clearly growing

more and more uncomfortable. "I have some written material with me. If you want, you can read it."

"I don't want to read right now; I want you to explain it to me," I insisted.

He looked around for the wine bottle, but it was empty. Neither of us could remember why we had come to the well in the first place. Something important was in the air—as if what he was saying were part of a miracle.

"Go on," I urged him.

"Her symbol is water—like the fog all around us. The Goddess uses water as the means to manifest Herself."

The mist suddenly seemed to take on a life of its own, becoming sacred—even though I still didn't understand what he was trying to say.

"I don't want to talk to you about history. If you want to learn about the history, you can read the books I brought with me. But you should know that this woman—the Goddess, the Virgin Mary, the Shechinah, the Great Mother, Isis, Sofia, slave and mistress—is present in every religion on the face of the earth. She has been forgotten, prohibited, and disguised, but Her cult has continued from millennium to millennium and continues to survive today.

"One of the faces of God is the face of a woman."

I studied his face. His eyes were gleaming, and he was staring into the fog that enveloped us. I could see that I no longer needed to prompt him.

"She is present in the first chapter of the Bible—when the spirit of God hovered over the waters, and He placed them below and above the stars. It was the mystic marriage of earth and heaven. She is present in the final chapter of the Bible, when

> the Spirit and the bride say, "Come!"
> And let him who hears say, "Come!"
>
> And let him who thirsts come.
> Whoever desires, let him take the
> water of life freely."

"Why is water the symbol of the feminine face of God?"

"I don't know. But She normally chooses that medium to manifest Herself. Maybe because She is the source of life; we are generated in water, and for nine months we live in it. Water is the symbol of the power of woman, the power that no man—no matter how enlightened or perfect he may be—can capture."

He paused for a moment and then began again.

"In every religion and in every tradition, She manifests Herself in one form or another—She always manifests Herself. Since I am a Catholic, I perceive Her as the Virgin Mary."

He took me by the hand, and in less than five minutes, we had walked out of Saint-Savin. We passed a column by the side of the road that had something strange at the top: it was a cross with an image of the Virgin in the place where Jesus ought to have been.

Now the darkness and the mist completely enveloped us. I began to imagine I was immersed in water, in the maternal womb—where time and thought do not exist. Everything he had been saying to me was beginning to make sense. I remembered the woman at the conference. And then I thought of the girl who had led me to the plaza. She too had said that water was the symbol of the Goddess.

❧ ❧ ❧

TWENTY KILOMETERS from here there's a grotto," he was telling me. "On the eleventh of February, 1858, a young girl was baling hay near the grotto with two other children. She was a fragile, asthmatic girl who lived in miserable poverty. On that winter's day, she was afraid of crossing a small stream, because if she got wet she might fall ill. And her parents needed the little money she made as a shepherd.

"A woman dressed in white, with two golden roses on her feet, appeared. The woman treated the child as if she were a princess, asked if she might return to that place a certain number of times, and then vanished. The two other girls, who were entranced by what had happened, quickly spread the story.

"This brought on a long ordeal for the girl. She was imprisoned, and the authorities demanded that she deny the whole story. Others offered her money to get her to ask the apparition for special favors. Within days, her family began to be insulted in the plaza by people who thought that the girl had invented the story in order to get attention.

"The girl, whose name was Bernadette, had no understanding of what she had seen. She referred to the lady who had appeared as 'That,' and her parents, concerned as they were, went to the village priest for assistance.

The priest suggested that when the apparition next appeared, Bernadette should ask the woman's name.

"Bernadette did as she was asked, but received only a smile in response. 'That' appeared before her a total of eighteen times and, for the most part, said nothing. During one of her appearances, though, she asked the girl to kiss the ground. Without understanding why, Bernadette did as she was asked. During another visitation, she asked the girl to dig a hole in the floor of the grotto. Bernadette obeyed, and there immediately appeared a hole filled with filthy water, because swine were kept there.

"'Drink the water,' the woman said.

"The water was so dirty that although Bernadette cupped it in her hands, she threw it away three times, afraid to bring it to her mouth. Finally she did, despite her repugnance. In the place where she had dug, more water began to come forth. A man who was blind in one eye applied several drops of the water to his face and recovered his vision. A woman, desperate because her newborn child appeared to be dying, dipped the child in the spring—on a day when the temperature had fallen below zero. And the child was cured.

"Little by little, the word spread, and thousands of people began to come to the place. The girl repeatedly asked the woman her name, but the woman merely smiled.

"Until one day, 'That' turned to Bernadette, and said, 'I am the Immaculate Conception.'

"Satisfied at last, the girl ran to tell the parish priest.

"'That cannot be,' he said. 'No one can be the tree and the fruit at the same time, my child. Go there, and throw holy water on her.'

"As far as the priest was concerned, only God could have existed from the very beginning—and God, as far as anyone could tell, was a man."

He paused for a long time.

"Bernadette threw holy water on 'That,' and the apparition smiled tenderly, nothing more.

"On the sixteenth of July, the woman appeared for the last time. Shortly after, Bernadette entered a convent, not knowing that she had changed forever the destiny of that small village near the grotto. The spring continued to flow, and miracles followed, one after the other.

"The story spread, first throughout France and later the world. The city grew and was transformed. Businesses sprang up everywhere. Hotels opened. Bernadette died and was buried in a place far from there, never knowing what had occurred.

"Some people who wanted to put the church in a bad light—and who knew that the Vatican was now acknowledging apparitions—began to invent false miracles that were later unmasked. The church reacted strongly: from a certain date on, it would accept as miracles only those phenomena that passed a rigorous series of examinations performed by medical and scientific commissions.

"But the water still flows, and the cures continue."

I heard something nearby; it frightened me, but he didn't seem to notice. The fog now had a life and a story of its own. I was thinking about everything he had told me, and I wondered how he knew all of this.

I thought about the feminine face of God. The man at my side had a soul filled with conflict. A short time ago, he had written to me that he wanted to enter a Catholic seminary, yet now he was thinking that God has a feminine face.

He was silent. I still felt as if I were in the womb of the Earth Mother, beyond time and place.

"There were two important things that Bernadette didn't know," he finally said. "The first was that prior to the arrival of the Christian religion in these parts, these mountains were inhabited by Celts—and the Goddess was their principal object of devotion. Generations and generations had understood the feminine face of God and shared in Her love and Her glory."

"And the second thing?"

"The second was that a short time before Bernadette experienced her visions, the authorities at the Vatican had met in secret. Virtually no one knew what had occurred at those meetings—and there's no question but that the priest in the small village didn't have the slightest idea. The highest council of the Catholic Church was deciding whether they should ratify the dogma regarding the Immaculate Conception.

"The dogma wound up being ratified, through the papal bull known as *Ineffabilis Deus*. But the general public never knew exactly what this meant."

"And what do you have to do with all this?" I asked.

"I am Her disciple. I have learned through Her." He seemed to be saying that She was the source of all his knowledge.

"You have seen Her?"

"Yes."

(9 (9 (9

WE RETURNED to the plaza and walked toward the church. I saw the well in the lamplight, with the bottle of wine and two glasses on its wall. *A couple of sweethearts must have been here,* I think. *Silent, allowing their hearts to speak to each other. And after their hearts had said all they had to say, they began to share the great mysteries.*

I felt that I was facing something quite serious and that I needed to learn everything I could from my experiences. For a few moments, I thought about my studies, about Zaragoza, and about the man I was hoping to find in my life—but all that seemed far away, clouded by the mists over Saint-Savin.

"Why did you tell me the story of Bernadette?" I asked.

"I don't know why exactly," he answered, without looking at me directly. "Maybe because we're not too far from Lourdes. Maybe because the day after tomorrow is the day of the Immaculate Conception. Or maybe it was because I wanted to show you that my world is not so solitary and mad as it may appear. There are others who are part of that world, and they believe in what they say."

"I never said that your world is mad. Maybe it's mine that's crazy. I mean, here I am, spending the most crucial time of my life concentrating on textbooks and courses that won't help me at all to escape from the place I already know too well."

I sensed that he was relieved that I understood him. I expected him to say something more about the Goddess, but instead he turned to me and said, "Let's get some sleep. We've had a lot to drink."

Tuesday, December 7, 1993

❧ ❧ ❧

HE WENT straight to sleep, but I was awake for a long time, thinking about the fog, the wine, and our conversation. I read the manuscript he gave me, and what was in it thrilled me: God—if God really existed —was both Father and Mother.

Later, I turned out the light and lay there thinking. When we were quiet with each other, I was able to see how close I felt to him.

Neither of us had said anything. Love doesn't need to be discussed; it has its own voice and speaks for itself. That night, by the well, the silence had allowed our hearts to approach each other and get to know each other better. My heart had listened closely to what his had said, and now it was content.

Before I fell asleep, I decided I would do what he called the "exercise of the Other."

I am here in this room, I thought, *far from everything familiar to me, talking about things that have never interested me and sleeping in a city where I've never set foot before. I can pretend—at least for a few minutes—that I am different.*

I began to imagine how I would like to be living right at that moment. I wanted to be happy, curious, joyful—living every moment intensely, drinking the water of life thirstily. Believing again in my dreams. Able to fight for what I wanted.

Loving a man who loved me.

Yes, that was the woman I wanted to be—the woman who was suddenly presenting herself and becoming me.

I felt that my soul was bathed in the light of a god—or of a goddess—in whom I had lost faith. And I felt that at that moment, the Other left my body and was standing in the corner of that small room.

I observed the woman I had been up until then: weak but trying to give the impression of strength. Fearful of everything but telling herself it wasn't fear—it was the wisdom of someone who knew what reality was. Putting up shutters in front of windows to keep the joy of the sun from entering—just so the sun's rays wouldn't fade my old furniture.

I looked at the Other, there in the corner of the room—fragile, exhausted, disillusioned. Controlling and enslaving what should really be free: her emotions. Trying to judge her future loves by the rules of her past suffering.

But love is always new. Regardless of whether we love once, twice, or a dozen times in our life, we always face a brand-new situation. Love can consign us to hell or to paradise, but it always takes us somewhere. We simply have to accept it, because it is what nourishes our existence. If we reject it, we die of hunger, because we lack the courage to stretch out a hand and pluck the fruit from the branches of the tree of life. We have to take love where we find it, even if that means hours, days, weeks of disappointment and sadness.

The moment we begin to seek love, love begins to seek us.

And to save us.

When the Other left me, my heart once again began to speak to me. It told me that the breach in the dike had allowed the waters to pour through, that the wind was blowing in all directions at once, and that it was happy because I was once again willing to listen to what it had to say.

My heart told me that I was in love. And I fell asleep with a smile on my lips.

⟨⟩ ⟨⟩ ⟨⟩

WHEN I AWOKE, the window was open and he was gazing at the mountains in the distance. I watched him without saying anything, ready to close my eyes if he turned toward me.

As if he knew, he turned and looked at me.

"Good morning," he said.

"Good morning. Close the window—it's so cold."

The Other had appeared with no warning. It was still trying to change the direction of the wind, to detect shortcomings, to say, No, that's impossible. But it knew it was too late.

"I have to get dressed," I said.

"I'll wait for you downstairs."

I got up, banished the Other from my thoughts, opened the window again, and let the sun in. Its light bathed everything—the mountains with their snow-covered peaks, the ground blanketed in dry leaves, and the river, which I could hear but not see.

The sun shone on me, warming my nude body. I was no longer cold—I was consumed by a heat, the heat of a spark becoming a flame, the flame becoming a bonfire, the bonfire becoming an inferno. I knew.

I wanted this.

I also knew that from this moment on I was going to experience heaven and hell, joy and pain, dreams and hopelessness; that I would no longer be capable of containing the winds that blew from the hidden corners of my soul. I knew that from this moment on love would be my guide—and that it had waited to lead me ever since childhood, when I had felt love for the first time. The truth is, I had never forgotten love, even when it had deemed me unworthy of fighting for it. But love had been difficult, and I had been reluctant to cross its frontiers.

I recalled the plaza in Soria and the moment when I had asked him to find the medal I had lost. I had known what he was going to tell me, and I hadn't wanted to hear it, because he was the type who would someday go off in search of wealth, adventure, and dreams. I needed a love that was possible.

I realized that I had known nothing of love before. When I saw him at the conference and accepted his invitation, I'd thought that I, as a mature woman, would be able to control the heart of the girl who had been looking for so long for her prince. Then he had spoken about the child in all of us—and I'd heard again the voice of the child I had been, of the princess who was fearful of loving and losing.

For four days, I had tried to ignore my heart's voice, but it had grown louder and louder, and the Other had become desperate. In the furthest corner of my soul, my true self still existed, and I still believed in my dreams. Before the Other could say a word, I had accepted the ride with him. I had accepted the invitation to travel with him and to take the risks involved.

And because of that—because of that small part of me that had survived—love had finally found me, after it had looked for me everywhere. Love had found me, despite the barricade that the Other had built across a quiet street in Zaragoza, a barricade of preconceived ideas, stubborn opinions, and textbooks.

I opened the window and my heart. The sun flooded the room, and love inundated my soul.

ʕ ʕ ʕ

WE WANDERED FOR HOURS, through the snow and along the roads. We breakfasted in a village whose name I never found out but in whose central plaza a dramatic fountain sculpture displayed a serpent and a dove combined into a single fabulous creature.

He smiled when he saw it. "It's a sign—masculine and feminine joined in a single figure."

"I'd never thought before about what you told me yesterday," I said. "But it makes sense."

"'And God created man and woman,'" he quoted from Genesis, "because that was his image and simulacrum: man and woman."

I noted a new gleam in his eye. He was happy and laughed at every silly thing. He fell into easy conversation with the few people we met along the way—workers dressed in gray on their way to the fields, adventurers in colorful gear, preparing to climb a mountain peak. I said little—my French is awful—but my soul rejoiced at seeing him this way.

His joy made everyone who spoke with him smile. Perhaps his heart had spoken to him, and now he knew that I loved him—even though I was still behaving like just an old friend.

"You seem happier," I said at one point.

"Because I've always dreamed of being here with you, walking through these mountains and harvesting the 'golden fruits of the sun.'"

The golden fruits of the sun—a verse written ages ago, repeated by him now, at just the right moment.

"There's another reason you're happy," I said, as we left the small village with the strange statue.

"What's that?"

"You know that I'm happy. You're responsible for my being here today, climbing the mountains of truth, far from my mountains of notebooks and texts. You're making me happy. And happiness is something that multiplies when it is divided."

"Did you do the exercise of the Other?"

"Yes. How did you know?"

"Because you've changed too. And because we always learn that exercise at the right time."

The Other pursued me all through the morning. Every minute, though, its voice grew fainter, and its image seemed to dissolve. It reminded me of those vampire films where the monster crumbles into dust.

We passed another column with an image of the Virgin on the cross.

"What are you thinking about?" he asked me.

"About vampires. Those creatures of the night, locked inside themselves, desperately seeking company. Incapable of loving."

"That's why legend has it that only a stake through the heart can kill them; when that happens, the heart bursts, freeing the energy of love and destroying the evil."

"I never thought of that before. But it makes sense."

I had succeeded in burying the stake. My heart, freed of all its curses, was aware of everything. The Other no longer had a place to call its own.

A thousand times I wanted to take his hand, and a thousand times I stopped myself. I was still confused—I wanted to tell him I loved him, but I didn't know how to begin.

We talked about the mountains and the rivers. We were lost in a forest for almost an hour, but eventually we found the path again. We ate sandwiches and drank melted snow. When the sun began to set, we decided to return to Saint-Savin.

ŋ ŋ ŋ

THE SOUND of our footsteps echoed from the stone walls. At the entrance to the church, I instinctively dipped my hand in the font of holy water and made the sign of the cross. I recalled that water was the symbol of the Goddess.

"Let's go in," he suggested.

We walked through the dark, empty building. Saint Savin, a hermit who had lived at the start of the first millennium, was buried below the main altar. The walls of the place were crumbling and had clearly been reconstructed several times.

Some places are like that: they can suffer through wars, persecutions, and indifference, but they still remain sacred. Finally someone comes along, senses that something is missing, and rebuilds them.

I noticed an image of the crucified Christ that gave me a funny feeling—I had the impression that his head was moving, following me.

"Let's stop here."

We were before an altar of Our Lady.

"Look at the image."

Mary, with her son in her lap. The infant Jesus pointing to the heavens.

"Look more carefully," he said.

I studied the details of the wooden carving: the gilt paint, the pedestal, the perfection with which the artist had traced the folds of the robe. But it was when I focused on the finger of the child Jesus that I understood what he meant.

Although Mary held him in her arms, it was Jesus who was supporting her. The child's arm, raised to the sky, appeared to be lifting the Virgin toward heaven, back to the place of Her Groom's abode.

"The artist who created this more than six hundred years ago knew what he wanted to convey," he commented.

Footsteps sounded on the wooden floor. A woman entered and lit a candle in front of the main altar.

We remained silent for a while, respecting her moment of prayer.

Love never comes just a little at a time, I thought, as I watched him, absorbed in contemplation of the Virgin. The previous day, the world had made sense, even without love's presence. But now we needed each other in order to see the true brilliance of things.

When the woman had gone, he spoke again. "The artist knew the Great Mother, the Goddess, and the sympathetic face of God. You've asked me a question that up until now I haven't been able to answer directly. It was 'Where did you learn all this?' "

Yes, I had asked him that, and he had already answered me. But I didn't say so.

"Well, I learned in the same way that this artist did: I accepted love from on high. I allowed myself to be guided," he went on. "You must remember the letter I wrote you, when I spoke of wanting to enter a monastery. I never told you, but I did in fact do that."

I immediately remembered the conversation we'd had before the conference in Bilbao. My heart began to beat faster, and I tried to fix my gaze on the Virgin. She was smiling.

It can't be, I thought. *You entered and then you left. Please, tell me that you left the monastery.*

"I had already lived some pretty wild years," he said, not guessing my thoughts this time. "I got to see other peoples and other lands. I had already looked for God in the four corners of the earth. I had fallen in love with other women and worked in a number of different jobs."

Another stab. I would have to be careful that the Other didn't return. I kept my gaze on the Virgin's smile.

"The mysteries of life fascinated me, and I wanted to understand them better. I looked for signs that would tell me that someone knew something. I went to India and to Egypt. I sat with masters of magic and of meditation. And finally I discovered what I was looking for: that truth resides where there is faith."

Truth resides where there is faith! I looked around again at the interior of the church—the worn stones, fallen and replaced so many times. What had made human beings so insistent? What had caused them to work so hard at rebuilding this small temple in such a remote spot, hidden in the mountains?

Faith.

"The Buddhists were right, the Hindus were right, the Muslims were right, and so were the Jews. Whenever someone follows the path to faith—sincerely follows it—he or she is able to unite with God and to perform miracles.

"But it wasn't enough simply to know that—you have to make a choice. I chose the Catholic Church because I was raised in it, and my childhood had been impregnated with its mysteries. If I had been born Jewish, I would have chosen Judaism. God is the same, even though He has a thousand names; it is up to us to select a name for Him."

Once again, steps sounded in the church.

♔ ♔ ♔

A MAN APPROACHED and stared at us. Then he turned to the center altar and reached for the two candelabra. He must have been the one responsible for guarding the church.

I remembered the watchman at the other chapel, the man who wouldn't allow us to enter. But this man said nothing.

"I have a meeting tonight," he said when the man left.

"Please, go on with what you were saying. Don't change the subject."

"I entered a monastery close to here. For four years, I studied everything I could. During that time, I made contact with the Clarifieds and the Charismatics, the sects that have been trying to open doors that have been closed for so long to certain spiritual experiences. I discovered that God was not the ogre that had frightened me as a child. There was a movement afoot for a return to the original innocence of Christianity."

"You mean that after two thousand years, they finally understood that it was time to allow Jesus to become a part of the church?" I said with some sarcasm.

"You may think you're joking, but that was exactly it. I began to study with one of the superiors at the monastery. He taught me that we have to accept the fire of revelation, the Holy Spirit."

The Virgin continued to smile, and the infant Jesus kept his joyful expression, but my heart stopped when he said that. I too had believed in that once—but time, age, and the feeling that I was a logical and practical person had distanced me from religion. I realized how much I wanted to recover my childhood faith, when I had believed in angels and miracles. But I couldn't possibly bring it back simply through an act of will.

"The superior told me that if I believed that I knew, then I would in fact eventually know," he continued. "I began to talk to myself when I was in my cell. I prayed that the Holy Spirit would manifest itself and teach me what I needed to know. Little by little, I discovered that as I talked to myself, a wiser voice was saying things for me."

"That's happened to me, too," I interrupted him.

He waited for me to go on. But I couldn't say anything else.

"I'm listening," he said.

Something had stopped my tongue. He was speaking so beautifully, and I couldn't express myself nearly as well.

"The Other wants to come back," he said, as if he had guessed what I was thinking. "The Other is always afraid of saying something that might sound silly."

"Yes," I said, struggling to overcome my fear. "OK, sometimes when I'm talking with someone and get excited about what I'm saying, I find myself saying things I've never said before. It seems almost as if I'm 'channeling' an intelligence that isn't mine—one that understands life much better than me. But this is rare. In most conversations I prefer to listen. I always feel as if I'm learning something new, even though I wind up forgetting it all."

"We are our own greatest surprise," he said. "Faith as tiny as a grain of sand allows us to move mountains. That's what I've learned. And now, my own words sometimes surprise me.

"The apostles were fishermen, illiterate and ignorant. But they accepted the flame that fell from the heavens. They were not ashamed of their own ignorance; they had faith in the Holy Spirit. This gift is there for anyone who will accept it. One has only to believe, accept, and be willing to make mistakes."

The Virgin smiled down on me. She had every reason to cry—but She was joyful.

"Go on."

"That's all," he answered. "Accept the gift. And then the gift manifests itself."

"It doesn't work that way."

"Didn't you understand me?"

"I understand. But I'm like everyone else: I'm scared. It might work for you or for my neighbor, but never for me."

"That will change someday—when you begin to see that we are really just like that child there."

"But until then, we'll all go on thinking we've come close to the light, when actually we can't even light our own flame."

He didn't answer.

"You didn't finish your story about the seminary," I said.

"I'm still there."

Before I could react, he stood up and walked to the center of the church.

I stayed where I was. My head was spinning. *Still in the seminary?*

Better not to think about it. Love had flooded my soul, and there was no way I could control it. There was only one recourse: the Other, with whom I had been harsh because I was weak, and cold because I was afraid—but I no longer wanted the Other. I could no longer look at life through its eyes.

A sharp, sustained sound like that of an immense flute interrupted my thoughts. My heart jumped.

The sound came again. And again. I looked behind me and saw a wooden staircase that led up to a crude platform, which didn't seem to fit with the frozen beauty of the church. On the platform was an ancient organ.

And there he was. I couldn't see his face because the lighting was bad—but I knew he was up there.

I stood up, and he called to me.

"Pilar!" he said, his voice full of emotion. "Stay where you are."

I obeyed.

"May the Great Mother inspire me," he said. "May this music be my prayer for the day."

And he began to play the Ave Maria. It must have been about six in the evening, time for the Angelus—a time when light and darkness merge. The sound of the organ echoed through the empty church, blending in my mind with the stones and the images laden with history and with faith. I closed my eyes and let the music flow through me, cleansing my soul of all fear and sin and reminding me that I am always better than I think and stronger than I believe.

For the first time since I had abandoned the path of faith, I felt a strong desire to pray. Although I was seated in a pew, my soul was kneeling at the feet of the Lady before me, the woman who had said,

"*Yes,*"

when She could have said "no." The angel would have sought out someone else, and there would have been no sin in the eyes of the Lord, because God knows His children's weakness.

But She had said,

"*Thy will be done,*"

even though She sensed that She was receiving, along with the words of the angel, all the pain and suffering of Her destiny; even though Her heart's eyes could see Her beloved son leaving the house, could see the people who would follow Him and then deny Him; but

"*Thy will be done,*"

even when, at the most sacred moment in a woman's life, She had to lie down with the animals in a stable to give birth, because that was what the Scriptures required;

"*Thy will be done,*"

even when, in agony, She looked through the streets for Her son and found Him at the temple. And He asked that She not interfere because He had other obligations and tasks to perform;

"Thy will be done,"

even when She knew that She would search for Him for the rest of Her days, Her heart filled with pain, fearing every moment for His life, knowing that He was being persecuted and threatened;

"Thy will be done,"

even when, finding Him in the crowd, She was unable to draw near Him;

"Thy will be done,"

even when She asked someone to tell Him that She was there and the son sent back the response, "My mother and my brothers are those who are here with me";

"Thy will be done,"

even when at the end, after everyone had fled, only She, another woman, and one of them stood at the foot of the cross, bearing the laughter of His enemies and the cowardice of His friends;

"Thy will be done."

Thy will be done, my Lord. Because you know the weakness in the heart of your children, and you assign each of them only the burden they can bear. May you understand my love—because it is the only thing I have that is really mine, the only thing that I will be able to take with me into the next life. Please allow it to be courageous and pure; please make it capable of surviving the snares of the world.

The organ stopped, and the sun went into hiding behind the mountains—as if both were ruled by the same Hand. The music had been his prayer, and his prayer had been heard. I opened my eyes and found the church in complete darkness, except for the solitary candle that illuminated the image of the Virgin.

I heard his footsteps again, returning to where I sat. The light of that single candle gleamed on my tears, and my smile—a smile that wasn't perhaps as beautiful as the Virgin's—showed that my heart was alive.

He looked at me, and I at him. My hand reached out for his and found it. Now it was his heart that was beating faster—I could almost hear it in the silence.

But my soul was serene, and my heart at peace.

I held his hand, and he embraced me. We stood there at the feet of the Virgin for I don't know how long. Time had stopped.

She looked down at us. The adolescent girl who had said "yes" to her destiny. The woman who had agreed to carry the son of God in Her womb and the love of God in Her heart. She understood.

I didn't want to ask for anything. That afternoon in the church had made the entire journey worthwhile. Those four days with him had made up for an entire year in which so little had happened.

We left the church hand in hand and walked back toward our room. My head was spinning—seminary, Great Mother, the meeting he had later that night.

I realized then that we both wanted to unite our souls under one destiny—but the seminary and Zaragoza stood in the way. My heart felt squeezed. I looked around at the medieval homes and the well where we had sat the previous night. I recalled the silence and the sadness of the Other, the woman I had once been.

God, I am trying to recover my faith. Please don't abandon me in the middle of this adventure, I prayed, pushing my fears aside.

❧　❧　❧

HE SLEPT A LITTLE, but I stayed awake, looking out the darkened window. Later, we got up and dined with the family—they never spoke at the table. He asked for a key to the house.

"We'll be home late tonight," he said to the woman.

"Young people should enjoy themselves," she answered, "and take advantage of the holidays as best they can."

"I have to ask you something," I said, when we were back in the car. "I've been trying to avoid it, but I have to ask."

"The seminary," he said.

That's right. I don't understand. Even though it's no longer important, I thought.

"I have always loved you," he began. "I kept the medal, thinking that someday I would give it to you and that I'd have the courage to tell you that I love you. Every road I traveled led back to you. I wrote the letters to you and opened every letter of yours afraid that you would tell me you had found someone.

"Then I was called to the spiritual life. Or rather, I accepted the call, because it had been with me since childhood—just as it was for you. I discovered that God was extremely important to my life and that I couldn't be happy if I didn't accept my vocation. The face of Christ was there in the face of every poor soul I met on my travels, and I couldn't deny it."

He paused, and I decided not to push him.

Twenty minutes later, he stopped the car and we got out.

"This is Lourdes," he said. "You should see it during the summer."

What I saw now were deserted streets, closed shops, and hotels with bars across their entrances.

"Six million people come here in the summer," he went on enthusiastically.

"It looks like a ghost town to me."

We crossed a bridge and arrived at an enormous iron gate with angels on either side. One side of the gate was standing open, and we passed through it.

"Go on with what you were saying," I said, in spite of my decision not to pursue it. "Tell me about the face of Christ on the people you met."

I could see that he didn't want to continue the conversation. Perhaps this wasn't the right time or place. But having begun, he had to complete it.

We were walking down a broad avenue, bordered on both sides by snow-covered fields. At its end, I could see the silhouette of a cathedral.

"Go on," I repeated.

"You already know. I entered the seminary. During the first year, I asked that God help me to transform my love for you into a love for all people. In the second year, I sensed that God had heard me. By the third year, even though my longing for you was still strong, I became certain that my love was turning toward charity, prayer, and helping the needy."

"Then why did you seek me out? Why rekindle the flame in me? Why did you tell me about the exercise of the Other and force me to see how shallow my life is?" I sounded confused and tremulous. From one minute to the next, I could see him drawing closer to the seminary and further from me. "Why did you come back? Why wait until today to tell me this story, when you can see that I am beginning to love you?"

He did not answer immediately. Then he said, "You'll think it's stupid."

"I won't. I'm not worried anymore about seeming ridiculous. You've taught me that."

"Two months ago, my superior asked me to accompany him to the house of a woman who had died and left all her wealth to the seminary. She lived in Saint-Savin, and my superior had to prepare an inventory of what was there."

We were approaching the cathedral at the end of the avenue. My intuition told me that as soon as we reached it, any conversation we were having would be interrupted.

"Don't stop," I said. "I deserve an explanation."

"I remember the moment I stepped into that house. The windows looked out on the Pyrenees, and the whole scene was filled with the brightness of the sun, intensified by the snow's glare. I began to make a list of the things in the house, but after just a few minutes, I had to stop.

"I had discovered that the woman's taste was exactly the same as mine. She owned records that I would have purchased, the same music that I would have enjoyed listening to as I looked out on that beautiful landscape. Her bookshelves were filled with books I had already read and others that I would have loved to read. Looking at the furnishings, the paintings, and all her other possessions, I felt as if I had chosen them myself.

"From that day on, I couldn't forget that house. Every time I went to the chapel to pray, I realized that my renunciation had not been total. I imagined myself there with you, looking out at the snow on the mountaintops, a fire blazing in the hearth. I pictured our children running around the house and playing in the fields around Saint-Savin."

Although I had never been near the house, I knew exactly what it looked like. And I hoped he'd say nothing else so that I could fantasize.

But he went on.

"For the past two weeks, I haven't been able to stand the sadness in my soul. I went to my superior and told him what was happening to me. I told him about my love for you and what had begun when we were taking the inventory."

A light rain began to fall. I bowed my head and gathered the front of my coat. I suddenly didn't want to hear the rest of the story.

"So my superior said, 'There are many ways to serve our Lord. If you feel that's your destiny, go in search of it. Only a man who is happy can create happiness in others.'

" 'I don't know if that's my destiny,' I told my superior. 'Peace came into my heart when I entered this seminary.'

" 'Well, then, go there and resolve any doubts you may have,' he said. 'Remain out there in the world, or come back to the seminary. But you have to be committed to the place you choose. A divided kingdom cannot defend itself from its adversaries. A divided person cannot face life in a dignified way.' "

He pulled something from his pocket and handed it to me. It was a key.

"The superior loaned me the key to the house. He said that he would hold off for a while on selling the possessions. I know that he wants me to return to the seminary. But he was the one who arranged the presentation in Madrid—so that we could meet."

I looked at the key in my hand and smiled. In my heart, bells were ringing, and the heavens had opened to me. He could serve God in a different way—by my side. Because I was going to fight for that to happen.

I put the key in my bag.

❧ ❧ ❧

THE BASILICA LOOMED in front of us. Before I could say anything, someone spotted him and came toward us. The light rain continued, and I had no idea how long we would be there; I couldn't forget that I had only one set of clothes, and I didn't want them to get soaked.

I concentrated on that problem. I didn't want to think about the house—that was a matter suspended between heaven and earth, awaiting the hand of destiny.

He introduced me to several people who had gathered around. They asked where we were staying, and when he said Saint-Savin, one of them told us the story of the hermit saint who was buried there. It was Saint Savin who had discovered the well in the middle of the plaza—and the original mission of the village had been to create a refuge for religious persons who had left the city and come to the mountains in search of God.

"They are still living there," another said.

I didn't know if the story was true, nor did I have any idea who "they" were.

Other people began to arrive, and the group began to move toward the entrance of the grotto. An older man tried to tell me something in French. When he saw that I didn't understand, he switched to an awkward Spanish.

"You are with a very special man," he said. "A man who performs miracles."

I said nothing but remembered that night in Bilbao when a desperate man had come looking for him. He had told me nothing about where he had gone, and I hadn't asked. Right now, I preferred to think about the house, which I could picture perfectly—its books, its records, its view, its furniture.

Somewhere in the world, a home awaited us. A place where we could care for daughters or sons who would come home from school, fill the house with joy, and never pick up after themselves.

We walked in silence through the rain until finally we reached the place where the visions of Mary had occurred. It was exactly as I had imagined: the grotto, the statue of Our Lady, and the fountain—protected by glass—where the miracle of the water had taken place. Some pilgrims were praying; others were seated silently inside the grotto, their eyes closed. A river ran past the entrance, and the sound of the water made me feel at peace. As soon as I saw the image, I said a quick prayer, asking the Virgin to help me—my heart needed no more suffering.

If pain must come, may it come quickly. Because I have a life to live, and I need to live it in the best way possible. If he has to make a choice, may he make it now. Then I will either wait for him or forget him.

Waiting is painful. Forgetting is painful. But not knowing which to do is the worst kind of suffering.

In some corner of my heart, I felt that she had heard my plea.

Wednesday, December 8, 1993

✿ ✿ ✿

BY THE TIME the cathedral's clock struck midnight, the group around us had grown considerably. We were almost a hundred people—some of them priests and nuns—standing in the rain, gazing at the statue.

"Hail, Our Lady of the Immaculate Conception," someone close to me said, as soon as the tolling of the bells ceased.

"Hail," everyone answered, with some applause.

A guard immediately came forward and asked that we be quiet. We were bothering the other pilgrims.

"But we've come a long way," said one of the men in our group.

"So have they," answered the guard, pointing to the others who were praying in the rain. "And they are praying silently."

I wanted to be alone with him, far from this place, holding his hand and telling him how I felt. We needed to talk more about the house, about our plans, about love. I wanted to reassure him, to make clear how strong my feelings were, and to let him know that his dream could come true—because I would be at his side, helping him.

The guard retreated, and one of the priests began to recite the rosary in a low voice. When we reached the creed that closes the series of prayers, everyone remained silent, their eyes closed.

"Who are these people?" I asked.

"Charismatics," he answered.

I had heard of them before but didn't know exactly what their name meant. He could see that I didn't understand.

"These are people who accept the fire of the Holy Spirit," he said, "the fire that Jesus left but that is used by so few people to light their candles. These people are very close to the original truth of Christianity, when everyone was capable of performing miracles.

"They are guided by the Woman Dressed by the Sun," he said, pointing with his eyes to the Virgin.

The group began to chant quietly, as if in response to an invisible command.

"You're shivering from the cold. You don't have to take part in this," he said.

"Are you going to stay?"

"Yes. This is my life."

"Then I'm going to participate," I answered, even though I would have preferred to be far from there. "If this is your world, I want to learn to be a part of it."

The group continued to sing. I closed my eyes and tried to follow the words, even though I couldn't speak French. I repeated the words without understanding them. But their sound helped the time to pass more quickly.

It would end soon. And we could return to Saint-Savin, just the two of us.

I went on singing mechanically—but little by little, I began to feel the music taking hold of me, as if it had a life of its own. It was hypnotizing. The cold seemed less bitter, and the rain no longer bothered me. The music made me feel better. It transported me back to a time when God had felt closer to me and had helped me.

Just as I was about to surrender completely to the music, it stopped.

I opened my eyes. This time, instead of a guard, there was a priest. He approached one of the other priests in our group. They whispered to one another for a few moments, and the padre left.

Our priest turned to us. "We have to say our prayers on the other side of the river," he said.

๓ ๓ ๓

SILENTLY, WE WALKED across the bridge directly in front of the grotto and moved to the other bank. It was a prettier place, on the bank of the river, surrounded by trees and an open field. The river now separated us from the grotto. From there, we could clearly see the illuminated image, and we could sing loudly without disturbing others' prayers.

The people around me began to sing louder, raising their faces to the sky and smiling as the raindrops coursed down their cheeks. Some raised their arms, and soon everyone joined in, waving their arms from side to side in rhythm to the music.

I wanted to give in to the moment, but at the same time I wanted to pay close attention to what they were doing. One priest near me was singing in Spanish, and I tried to repeat the words. They were invocations to the Holy Spirit and the Virgin, requesting their presence and asking that they rain down their blessings and their powers on each of us.

"May the gift of tongues befall us," said another priest, repeating the phrase in Spanish, Italian, and French.

What happened next was incomprehensible. Each of the many people present began to speak a language that was different from any I had ever heard. It was more sound than speech, with words that seemed to come straight from the soul, making no sense at all. I recalled our conversation in the church, when he had spoken about revelations, saying that all wisdom was the result of listening to one's own soul. *Perhaps this is the language of the angels,* I thought, trying to mimic what they were doing—and feeling ridiculous.

Everyone was looking at the statue of the Virgin on the other side of the river; they all seemed to be in a trance. I looked around for him and found him standing at some distance from me. His hands were raised to the heavens and he was speaking rapidly, as if in conversation with Her. He was smiling and nodding his head as if in agreement; occasionally he looked surprised.

This is his world, I thought.

The whole scene began to scare me. The man I wanted at my side was telling me that God is also female, he was speaking an incomprehensible language, he was in a trance, and he seemed closer to the angels than to me. The house in the mountains began to seem less real, as if it were part of a world that he had already left behind.

All of our days together—starting with the conference in Madrid—seemed to be part of a dream, a voyage beyond the space and time of my life. At the same time, though, the dream had the flavor of the world, of romance, and of new adventures. I had tried to resist; now I knew how easily love could set fire to the heart. I had tried to stay unreceptive to all of this in the beginning; now I felt that since I had loved before, I would know how to handle it.

I looked around again, and it dawned on me that this was not the Catholicism I had been taught at school. And this was not the way I had pictured the man in my life.

A man in my life! How strange! I said to myself, surprised at the thought.

There on the bank of the river, looking across at the grotto, I felt both fear and jealousy. Fear because it was all new to me, and what is new has always scared me. Jealousy because, bit by bit, I could see that his love was greater than I'd thought and spread over places where I'd never set foot.

Forgive me, Our Lady. Forgive me if I'm being selfish or small-minded, competing with you for this man's love.

But what if his vocation wasn't to be with me but was to retreat from the world, locking himself in a seminary and conversing with angels? How long would he resist before he fled from our house to return to his true path? Or even if he never went back to the seminary, what price would I have to pay to keep him from returning to that path?

Everyone there, except me, seemed to be concentrating on what they were doing. I was staring at him, and he was speaking the language of the angels.

Suddenly, fear and jealousy were replaced by calm and solitude. The angels had someone to talk with, and I was alone.

I had no idea what pushed me into trying to speak that strange language. Perhaps it was my strong need to connect with him, to tell him what I was feeling. Perhaps I needed to let my soul speak to me—my heart had so many doubts and needed so many answers.

I didn't know exactly what to do, and I felt ridiculous. But all around me were men and women of all ages, priests and laypeople, novices and nuns, students and old-timers. They gave me the courage to ask the Holy Spirit for the strength to overcome my fear.

Try, I said to myself. *All you have to do is open your mouth and have the courage to say things you don't understand. Try!*

I prayed that this night—the night following a day that had been so long that I couldn't even remember how it had begun—would be an epiphany. A new beginning for me.

God must have heard me. The words began to come more easily—and little by little they lost their everyday meanings. My embarrassment diminished, my confidence grew, and the words began to flow freely. Although I understood nothing of what I was saying, it all made sense to my soul.

Simply having the courage to say senseless things made me euphoric. I was free, with no need to seek or to give explanations for what I was doing. This freedom lifted me to the heavens—where a greater love, one that forgives everything and never allows you to feel abandoned, once again enveloped me.

It feels as if my faith is coming back, I thought, surprised at the miracles that love can perform. I sensed that the Virgin was holding me in her lap, covering me and warming me with her mantle. The strange words flew more rapidly from my lips.

Without realizing it, I began to cry. Joy flooded my heart—a joy that overpowered my fears and was stronger than my attempts to control every second of my life.

I realized that my tears were a gift; at school, the sisters had taught me that the saints wept with ecstasy. I opened my eyes, gazed at the darkness of the heavens, and felt my tears blending with the raindrops. The earth was alive and the drops from above brought the miracles of heaven with them. We were all a part of that same miracle.

How wonderful that God may be a woman, I said to myself, as the others continued to chant. *If that's true, then it was certainly God's feminine face that taught us how to love.*

"Let us pray in tents of eight," said the priest in Spanish, Italian, and French.

Once again, I was confused. What was happening? Someone came over to me and put his arm around my shoulders. Another person did the same on my other side. We formed a circle of eight people, arms around each other's shoulders. Then we leaned forward, our heads touching.

We looked like a human tent. The rain fell harder, but no one cared. The position we had taken concentrated all our energies and heat.

"May the Immaculate Conception help my child find his way," said the man embracing me from the right. "Please, let's say an Ave Maria for my child."

"Amen," everyone said. And we eight prayed an Ave Maria.

"May the Immaculate Conception enlighten me and arouse in me the gift of curing," said a woman from our circle. "Let us say an Ave Maria."

Again, all of us said "Amen" and we prayed. Each person made a petition, and everyone participated in the prayers. I was surprised at myself, because I was praying like a child—and like a child, I believed that our prayers would be answered.

The group fell silent for a fraction of a second. I realized that it was my turn to make a petition. Under any other circumstances, I would have died of embarrassment and been unable to say a word. But I felt a presence, and that presence gave me confidence.

"May the Immaculate Conception teach me to love as she loves," I finally said. "May that love grow in me and in the man to whom it is dedicated. Let us say an Ave Maria."

We prayed together, and again I felt a sense of freedom. For years, I had fought against my heart, because I was afraid of sadness, suffering, and abandonment. But now I knew that true love was above all that and that it would be better to die than to fail to love.

I had thought that only others had the courage to love. But now I discovered that I too was capable of loving. Even if loving meant leaving, or solitude, or sorrow, love was worth every penny of its price.

I have to stop thinking of these things. I have to concentrate on the ritual.

The priest leading the group asked that we disband the tents and pray for the sick. Everyone continued to pray, sing, and dance in the rain, adoring God and the Virgin Mary. Now and then, people went back to speaking strange languages, waving their arms, and pointing to the sky.

"Someone here . . . someone who has a sick daughter-in-law . . . must know that she is being cured," cried one woman.

The prayers resumed, along with chants of joy. From time to time, we would hear the voice of this woman again.

"Someone in this group who lost her mother recently must have faith and know that she is in the glory of heaven."

Later, he would tell me that she had the gift of prophecy, that certain individuals can sense what is happening at some distant place or what will happen in the future.

Secretly, I too believed in the power of that voice that was speaking of miracles. I hoped that voice would speak of the love between two of those present. I hoped to hear that voice proclaim that this love was blessed by all the angels and saints—and by God and by the Goddess.

ら   ら   ら

I'M NOT SURE how long the ritual lasted. People continued to speak in tongues and to chant; they danced with their arms held up to the sky, prayed for the people around them, and petitioned for miracles.

Finally, the priest who was conducting the ceremony said, "Let us chant a prayer for all of those here who are participating for the first time in a Charismatic renewal."

Apparently I was not the only one. That made me feel better.

Everyone chanted a prayer. This time I just listened, asking that favors be granted to me.

I needed many.

"Let us receive the blessing," said the priest.

The crowd turned toward the illuminated grotto across the river. The priest said several prayers and blessed us all. Then everyone kissed, wished each other a "Happy Day of the Immaculate Conception," and went their separate ways.

He came to me. His expression was happier than usual.

"You're soaked," he said.

"So are you!" I laughed.

We walked back to the car and drove to Saint-Savin. I'd been so eager for this moment to arrive—but now that it was here, I didn't know what to say. I couldn't even bring myself to talk about the house in the mountains, the ritual, the strange languages, or the tent prayers.

He was living in two worlds. Somewhere, those two worlds intersected—and I had to find where that was.

But at that moment, words were useless. Love can only be found through the act of loving.

"I've only got one sweater left," he said when we reached the room. "You can have it. I'll buy another for myself tomorrow."

"We'll put our wet things on the heater. They'll be dry by tomorrow. Anyway, I've got the blouse that I washed yesterday."

Neither of us said anything for a few minutes.

Clothing. Nakedness. Cold.

Finally, he took another shirt out of his bag. "You can sleep in this," he said.

"Great," I answered.

I turned out the light. In the dark, I took off my wet clothes, spread them over the heater, and turned it to high.

By the light from the lamppost outside the window, he must have been able to make out my silhouette and known that I was naked. I slipped the shirt on and crawled under the covers.

"I love you," I heard him say.

"I'm learning how to love you."

He lit a cigarette. "Do you think the right moment will come?" he asked.

I knew what he meant. I got up and sat on the edge of his bed.

The light from his cigarette illuminated our faces. He took my hand and we sat there for some time. I ran my fingers through his hair.

"You shouldn't have asked," I said. "Love doesn't ask many questions, because if we stop to think we become fearful. It's an inexplicable fear; it's difficult even to describe it. Maybe it's the fear of being scorned, of not being accepted, or of breaking the spell. It's ridiculous, but that's the way it is. That's why you don't ask—you act. As you've said many times, you have to take risks."

"I know. I've never asked before."

"You already have my heart," I told him. "Tomorrow you may go away, but we will always remember the miracle of these few days. I think that God, in Her infinite wisdom, conceals hell in the midst of paradise—so that we will always be alert, so that we won't forget the pain as we experience the joy of compassion."

He took my face in his hands. "You learn quickly," he said.

I had surprised myself. But sometimes if you think you know something, you do wind up understanding it.

"I hope you won't think I'm being difficult," I said. "I have been with many men. I've made love to some I've barely known."

"Same here," he said.

He was trying to sound natural, but from his touch, I could tell that he hadn't wanted to hear this from me.

"But since this morning, I feel as if I'm rediscovering love. Don't try to understand it, because only a woman would know what I mean. And it takes time."

He caressed my face. Then I kissed him lightly on the lips and returned to my bed.

I wasn't sure why I did. Was I trying to bind him even closer to me, or was I trying to set him free? In any case, it had been a long day, and I was too tired to think about it.

For me, that was a night of great peace. At one point, I seemed to be awake even though I was still sleeping. A feminine presence cradled me in Her lap; I felt as if I had known Her a long time. I felt protected and loved.

I woke at seven, dying of the heat. I remembered having turned the heater to high in order to dry my clothes. It was still dark, and I tried to get up without making a sound so that I wouldn't disturb him.

But as soon as I stood, I could see that he wasn't there.

I started to panic. The Other immediately awoke and said to me, "See? You agreed, and he disappeared. Like all men do."

My panic was increasing by the minute, but I didn't want to lose control. "I'm still here," the Other said. "You allowed the wind to change direction. You opened the door, and now love is flooding your life. If we act quickly, we'll be able to regain control."

I had to be practical, to take precautions.

"He's gone," said the Other. "You have to get away from this place in the middle of nowhere. Your life in Zaragoza is still intact; get back there quickly—before you lose everything you've worked so hard to gain."

He must have had some good reason, I thought.

"Men always have their reasons," said the Other. "But the fact is that they always wind up leaving."

Well, then, I had to figure out how to get back to Spain. I had to keep my wits about me.

"Let's start with the practical problem: money," the Other said.

I didn't have a cent. I would have to go downstairs, call my parents collect, and wait for them to wire me the money for a ticket home.

But it was a holiday, and the money wouldn't arrive until the next day. How would I eat? How would I explain to the owners of the house that they would have to wait for several days for their payment? "Better not to say anything," said the Other.

Right, she was the experienced one. She knew how to handle situations like this. She wasn't the impassioned girl who loses control of herself. She was the woman who always knew what she wanted in life. I should simply stay on there, as if he were expected to return. And when the money arrived, I would pay the bill and leave.

"Very good," said the Other. "You're getting back to how you were before. Don't be sad. One of these days, you'll find another man—one you can love without taking so many risks."

I gathered my clothes from the heater. They were dry. I needed to find out which of the surrounding villages had a bank, make a phone call, take steps. If I thought carefully about all of that, there wouldn't be time for crying or regrets.

Then I saw his note:

I've gone to the seminary. Pack up your things, because we're going back to Spain tonight. I'll be back by late afternoon. I love you.

I clutched the note to my breast, feeling miserable and relieved at the same time. I noticed that the Other had retreated.

I loved him. With every minute that passed, my love was growing and transforming me. I once again had faith in the future, and little by little, I was recovering my faith in God. All because of love.

I will not talk to my own darkness anymore, I promised myself, closing the door on the Other. *A fall from the third floor hurts as much as a fall from the hundredth.*

If I have to fall, may it be from a high place.

〔 〕 〔 〕 〔 〕

DON'T GO OUT hungry again," said the woman.
"I didn't realize you spoke Spanish," I answered,
surprised.

"The border isn't far from here. Tourists come to
Lourdes in the summer. If I couldn't speak Spanish,
I couldn't rent rooms."

She made me some toast and coffee. I was already
trying to prepare myself to make it through the day—
each hour was going to seem like a year. I hoped that
this snack would distract me for a while.

"How long have you two been married?" she asked.

"He was the first person I ever loved," I said. That was
enough.

"Do you see those peaks out there?" the woman continued. "The first love of my life died up in those
mountains."

"But you found someone else."

"Yes, I did. And I found happiness again. Fate is
strange: almost no one I know married the first love of
their lives. Those who did are always telling me that
they missed something important, that they didn't experience all that they might have."

She stopped talking suddenly. "I'm sorry," she said.
"I didn't mean to offend you."

"I'm not offended."

"I always look at that well there in the plaza. And I think to myself that before, no one knew where there was water. Then Saint Savin decided to dig and found it. If he hadn't done that, this village would be down there by the river."

"But what does that have to do with love?" I asked.

"That well brought many people here, with their hopes and dreams and conflicts. Someone dared to look for water, water was found, and people gathered where it flowed. I think that when we look for love courageously, it reveals itself, and we wind up attracting even more love. If one person really wants us, everyone does. But if we're alone, we become even more alone. Life is strange."

"Have you ever heard of the book called the *I Ching*?" I asked her.

"No, I haven't."

"It says that a city can be moved but not a well. It's around the well that lovers find each other, satisfy their thirst, build their homes, and raise their children. But if one of them decides to leave, the well cannot go with them. Love remains there, abandoned——even though it is filled with the same pure water as before."

"You speak like a mature woman who has already suffered a great deal, my dear," she said.

"No. I've always been frightened. I've never dug a well. But I'm trying to do that now, and I don't want to forget what the risks are."

I felt something in the pocket of my bag pressing at me. When I realized what it was, my heart went cold. I quickly finished my coffee.

The key. I had the key.

"There was a woman in this city who died and left everything to the seminary at Tarbes," I said. "Do you know where her house is?"

The woman opened the door and showed me. It was one of the medieval houses on the plaza. The back of the house looked out over the valley toward the mountains in the distance.

"Two priests went through the house about two months ago," she said. "And . . ." She stopped, looking at me doubtfully. "And one of them looked a lot like your husband."

"It was," I answered. The woman stood in her doorway, puzzled, as I quickly left. I felt a burst of energy, happy that I had allowed the child in me to pull a prank.

I soon stood in front of the house, not knowing what to do. The mist was everywhere, and I felt as if I were in a gray dream where strange figures might appear and take me away to places even more peculiar.

I toyed nervously with the key.

With the mist as thick as it was, it would be impossible to see the mountains from the window. The house would be dark; there would be no sun shining through the curtains. The house would seem sad without him at my side.

I looked at my watch. Nine in the morning.

I had to do something—something that would make the time pass, that would help me wait.

Wait. This was the first lesson I had learned about love. The day drags along, you make thousands of plans, you imagine every possible conversation, you promise to change your behavior in certain ways—and you feel more and more anxious until your loved one arrives. But by then, you don't know what to say. The hours of waiting have been transformed into tension, the tension has become fear, and the fear makes you embarrassed about showing affection.

I didn't know whether I should go in. I remembered our conversation of the previous day—the house was the symbol of a dream.

But I couldn't spend the whole day just standing there. I gathered up my courage, grasped the key firmly, and walked to the door.

ℓ ℓ ℓ

PILAR!"

The voice, with a strong French accent, came from the midst of the fog. I was more surprised than frightened. I thought it might be the owner of the house where we had rented the room—although I didn't recall having told him my name.

"Pilar!" I heard again, nearer this time.

I looked back at the plaza shrouded in mist. A figure was approaching, walking hurriedly. Perhaps the ghosts that I had imagined in the fog were becoming a reality.

"Wait," the figure said. "I want to talk to you."

When he had come closer, I could see that it was a priest. He looked like a caricature of the country padre: short, on the heavy side, with sparse white hair on a nearly bald head.

"Hola," he said, holding out his hand and smiling.

I answered him, a bit astonished.

"Too bad the fog is hiding everything," he said, looking toward the house. "Since Saint-Savin is in the mountains, the view from this house is beautiful; you can see the valley down below and the snow-covered peaks. But you probably already knew that."

I decided that this must be the superior from the monastery.

"What are you doing here?" I asked. "And how do you know my name?"

"Do you want to go in?" he said, trying to change the subject.

"No! I'd like you to answer my questions."

Rubbing his hands together to warm them, he sat down on the curb. I sat down next to him. The fog was growing thicker by the minute. The church was already hidden from sight, and it was only sixty feet away from us.

All I could see was the well. I remembered what the young woman in Madrid had said.

"She is present," I said.

"Who?"

"The Goddess," I answered. "She is this mist."

"So, he must have talked to you about that," he laughed. "Well, I prefer to refer to Her as the Virgin Mary. That's what I'm used to."

"What are you doing here? How do you know my name?" I repeated.

"I came here because I wanted to see you two. A member of the Charismatic group last night told me you were both staying in Saint-Savin. And it's a small place."

"He went to the seminary."

The padre's smile disappeared, and he shook his head. "Too bad," he said, as if speaking to himself.

"You mean, too bad he went to the seminary?"

"No, he's not there. I've just come from the seminary."

For a moment, I couldn't say anything. I thought back to the feeling I'd had when I woke up: the money, the arrangements I needed to make, the call to my parents, the ticket. But I'd made a vow, and I wasn't going to break it.

A priest was sitting beside me. As a child, I used to tell everything to our priest.

"I'm exhausted," I said, breaking the silence. "Less than a week ago, I finally learned who I am and what I want in life. Now I feel like I've been caught in a storm that's tossing me around, and I can't seem to do anything about it."

"Resist your doubts," the padre said. "It's important."

His advice surprised me.

"Don't be frightened," he continued, as if he knew what I was feeling. "I know that the church is in need of new priests, and he would be an excellent one. But the price he would have to pay would be very high."

"Where is he? Did he leave me here to return to Spain?"

"To Spain? There's nothing for him to do in Spain," said the priest. "His home is at the monastery, only a few kilometers from here. He's not there. But I know where we can find him."

His words brought back some of my joy and courage—at least he hadn't gone away.

But the priest was no longer smiling. "Don't let that encourage you," he went on, again reading my mind. "It would be better if he *had* gone back to Spain."

He stood and asked me to go with him. We could see only a few yards in front of us, but he seemed to know where he was going. We left Saint-Savin by the same road along which, two nights before—or could it have been five years before?—I had heard the story of Bernadette.

"Where are we going?" I asked.

"To find him," he answered.

"Padre, you've confused me," I said, as we walked along together. "You seemed sad when you said he wasn't at the seminary."

"Tell me what you know about the religious life, my child."

"Very little. Only that the priests take a vow of poverty, chastity, and obedience." I wondered whether I should go on and decided that I would. "And that they judge the sins of others, even though they may commit the same sins themselves. That they know all there is to know about marriage and love, but they never marry. That they threaten us with the fires of hell for mistakes that they themselves make. And they present God to us as a vengeful being who blames man for the death of His only Son."

The padre laughed. "You've had an excellent Catholic education," he said. "But I'm not asking you about Catholicism. I'm asking about the spiritual life."

I didn't respond for a moment. "I'm not sure. There are people who leave everything behind and go in search of God."

"And do they find Him?"

"Well, you would know the answer to that, Padre. I have no idea."

The padre noticed that I was beginning to gasp with exertion, and he slowed his pace.

"You had that wrong," he said. "A person who goes in search of God is wasting his time. He can walk a thousand roads and join many religions and sects—but he'll never find God that way.

"God is here, right now, at our side. We can see Him in this mist, in the ground we're walking on, even in my shoes. His angels keep watch while we sleep and help us in our work. In order to find God, you have only to look around.

"But meeting Him is not easy. The more God asks us to participate in His mysteries, the more disoriented we become, because He asks us constantly to follow our dreams and our hearts. And that's difficult to do when we're used to living in a different way.

"Finally we discover, to our surprise, that God wants us to be happy, because He is the father."

"And the mother," I said.

The fog was beginning to clear. I could see a small farmhouse where a woman was gathering hay.

"Yes, and the mother," he said. "In order to have a spiritual life, you need not enter a seminary, or fast, or abstain, or take a vow of chastity. All you have to do is have faith and accept God. From then on, each of us becomes a part of His path. We become a vehicle for His miracles."

"He has already told me about you," I interrupted, "and he has taught me these ideas."

"I hope that you accept God's gifts," he answered. "Because it hasn't always been that way, as history teaches us. Osiris was drawn and quartered in Egypt. The Greek gods battled because of the mortals on earth. The Aztecs expelled Quetzalcoatl. The Viking gods witnessed the burning of Valhalla because of a woman. Jesus was crucified. Why?"

I didn't have an answer.

"Because God came to earth to demonstrate His power to us. We are a part of His dream, and He wants His dream to be a happy one. Thus, if we acknowledge that God created us for happiness, then we have to assume that everything that leads to sadness and defeat is our own doing. That's the reason we always kill God, whether on the cross, by fire, through exile, or simply in our hearts."

"But those who understand Him . . ."

"They are the ones who transform the world—while making great sacrifices."

The woman carrying the hay saw the priest and came running in our direction. "Padre, thank you!" she said, kissing his hands. "The young man cured my husband!"

"It was the Virgin who cured your husband," he said. "The lad is only an instrument."

"It was he. Come in, please."

I recalled the previous night. When we arrived at the cathedral, a man had told me I was with a man who performed miracles.

"We're in a hurry," the padre said.

"No! No, we're not," I said, in my halting French. "I'm cold, and I'd like some coffee."

The woman took me by the hand, and we entered the house. It was simple but comfortable: stone walls, wood floors, and bare rafters. Seated in front of the fireplace was a man of about sixty. As soon as he saw the padre, he stood to kiss his hand.

"Don't get up," said the priest. "You still need to convalesce a bit."

"I've already gained twenty-five pounds," he answered. "But I'm still not able to be of much help to my wife."

"Not to worry. Before long, you'll be better than ever."

"Where is the young man?" the husband asked.

"I saw him heading toward where he always goes," the wife said. "Only today, he went by car."

The padre eyed me but didn't say anything.

"Give us your blessing, Père," the woman asked. "His power . . ."

"The Virgin's power," the priest corrected.

"The Virgin Mother's power is also your power, Père. It was you who brought it here."

This time, he didn't look my way.

"Pray for my husband, Père," the woman insisted.

The priest took a deep breath. "Stand in front of me," he said to the man.

The old man did as he was told. The padre closed his eyes and said an Ave Maria. Then he invoked the Holy Spirit, asking that it be present and help the man.

He suddenly began to speak rapidly. It sounded like a prayer of exorcism, although I couldn't understand what he was saying. His hands touched the man's shoulders and then slid down his arms to his fingertips. He repeated this gesture several times.

The fire began to crackle loudly in the fireplace. This may have been a coincidence, yet it seemed that the priest was entering into territory I knew nothing about—and that he was affecting the very elements.

Every snap of the fire startled the woman and me, but the padre paid no attention to it; he was completely involved in his task—an instrument of the Virgin, as he had said. He was speaking a strange language, and the words came forth at great speed. He was no longer moving his hands; they simply rested on the man's shoulders.

The ritual stopped as quickly as it had started. The padre turned and gave a conventional blessing, making the sign of the cross with his right hand. "May God be ever here in this house," he said.

And turning to me, he asked that we continue our walk.

"But you haven't had coffee," the woman said, as she saw that we were about to leave.

"If I have coffee now, I won't be able to sleep," the padre answered.

The woman laughed and murmured something like "It's still morning." But we were already on our way.

"Padre, the woman spoke of a young man who cured her husband. Was it he?"

"Yes, it was."

I began to feel uneasy. I remembered the day before, and Bilbao, and the conference in Madrid, and people speaking of miracles, and the presence that I had sensed as we embraced and prayed.

I was in love with a man who was capable of performing cures. A man who could help others, bring relief to suffering, give health to the sick and hope to their loved ones. Was I distracting him from his mission just because it was at odds with my image of a house with white curtains, cherished records, and favorite books?

"Don't blame yourself, my child," the padre said.

"You're reading my mind."

"Yes, I am," the padre said. "I have that gift too, and I try to be worthy of it. The Virgin taught me to penetrate the turmoil of human emotions in order to control them as well as possible."

"Do you perform miracles, too?"

"I am not able to cure. But I have one of the gifts of the Holy Spirit."

"So you can read my heart, Padre. And you know I love him, with a love that is growing every minute. We discovered the world together, and together we remain in it. He has been present every day of my life—whether I wanted him there or not."

What could I say to this priest who was walking beside me? He would never understand that I had had other men, that I had been in love, and that if I had married, I would be happy. Even as a child, I had found and forgotten love in the plaza of Soria.

But the way things looked now, I hadn't forgotten that first love very well. It had taken only three days for all of it to come rushing back.

"I have a right to be happy, Padre. I've recovered what was lost, and I don't want to lose it again. I'm going to fight for my happiness. If I give up the fight, I will also be renouncing my spiritual life. As you said, I would be putting God aside, along with my power and my strength as a woman. I'm going to fight for him, Padre."

I knew what that little man was doing here. He had come to convince me to leave him, because he had a more important mission to accomplish.

No, I couldn't believe that the padre walking at my side wanted us to marry and live in a house like the one in Saint-Savin. The priest had said that to trick me. He wanted me to lower my defenses and then—with a smile—he would convince me of the opposite.

He read my thoughts without saying a word. Or perhaps he was trying to fool me. Maybe he didn't know what others were thinking. The fog was dissipating rapidly, and I could now see the path, the mountain peak, the fields, and the snow-covered trees. My emotions were becoming clearer, as well.

Damn! If it's true that he can read someone's thoughts, then let him read mine and know everything! Let him know that yesterday he wanted to make love to me—that I refused and that now I regret it.

Yesterday I had thought that if he had to leave, I would still at least have the memory of my childhood friend. But that was nonsense. Even though he hadn't entered me, something even more profound had, and it had touched my heart.

"Padre, I love him," I repeated.

"So do I. And love always causes stupidity. In my case, it requires that I try to keep him from his destiny."

"That won't be easy, Padre. And it won't be easy in my case, either. Yesterday, during the prayers at the grotto, I discovered that I too can bring forth these gifts that you were talking about. And I'm going to use them to keep him with me."

"Good luck," said the padre, with a smile. "I hope you can."

He stopped and took a rosary from his pocket. Holding it, he looked into my eyes. "Jesus said that we should not take oaths, and I am not doing so. But I'm telling you, in the presence of all that is sacred to me, that I would not like him to adopt the conventional religious life. I would not like to see him ordained a priest. He can serve God in other ways—at your side."

It was hard for me to believe that he was telling me the truth. But he was.

"He's up there," the padre said.

I turned. I could see a car parked a bit further ahead—the same car we had driven from Spain.

"He always comes on foot," he said, smiling. "This time he wanted to give us the impression that he'd traveled a long way."

❧ ❧ ❧

THE SNOW WAS SOAKING my sneakers. But the padre was wearing only open sandals with woolen socks. I decided not to complain—if he could stand it, so could I. We began to hike toward the top of the mountains.

"How long will it take us?"

"Half an hour at the most."

"Where are we going?"

"To meet with him. And others."

I could see that he didn't want to say any more. Maybe he needed all of his energy for climbing. We walked along in silence—the fog had by now disappeared almost completely, and the yellow disk of the sun was coming into view.

For the first time I had a view of the entire valley; there was a river running through it, some scattered villages, and Saint-Savin, looking as though it were pasted against the slope of the mountain. I could make out the tower of the church, a cemetery I had not noticed before, and the medieval houses looking down on the river.

A bit below us, at a point we had already passed, a shepherd was tending his flock of sheep.

"I'm tired," the padre said. "Let's stop for a while."

We brushed the snow from the top of a boulder and rested against it. He was perspiring—and his feet must have been frozen.

"May Santiago preserve my strength, because I still want to walk his path one more time," said the padre, turning to me.

I didn't understand his comment, so I decided to change the subject. "There are footsteps in the snow."

"Some are those of hunters. Others are of men and women who want to relive a tradition."

"Which tradition?"

"The same as that of Saint Savin. Retreat from the world, come to these mountains, and contemplate the glory of God."

"Padre, there's something I need to understand. Until yesterday, I was with a man who couldn't choose between the religious life and marriage. Today, I learn that this same man performs miracles."

"We all perform miracles," he said. "Jesus said, 'If our faith is the size of a mustard seed, we will say to the mountain, "Move!" And it will move.'"

"I don't want a lesson in religion, Padre. I'm in love with a man, and I want to know more about him, understand him, help him. I don't care what everyone else can do or can't do."

The padre took a deep breath. He hesitated for a moment and then said, "A scientist who studied monkeys on an island in Indonesia was able to teach a certain one to wash bananas in the river before eating them.

Cleansed of sand and dirt, the food was more flavorful. The scientist—who did this only because he was studying the learning capacity of monkeys—did not imagine what would eventually happen. So he was surprised to see that the other monkeys on the island began to imitate the first one.

"And then, one day, when a certain number of monkeys had learned to wash their bananas, the monkeys on all of the other islands in the archipelago began to do the same thing. What was most surprising, though, was that the other monkeys learned to do so without having had any contact with the island where the experiment had been conducted."

He stopped. "Do you understand?"

"No," I answered.

"There are several similar scientific studies. The most common explanation is that when a certain number of people evolve, the entire human race begins to evolve. We don't know how many people are needed—but we know that's how it works."

"Like the story of the Immaculate Conception," I said. "The vision appeared for the wise men at the Vatican and for the simple farmer."

"The world itself has a soul, and at a certain moment, that soul acts on everyone and everything at the same time."

"A feminine soul."

He laughed, without saying just what he was laughing about.

"By the way, the dogma of the Immaculate Conception was not just a Vatican matter," he said. "Eight million people signed a petition to the pope, asking that it be recognized. The signatures came from all over the world."

"Is that the first step, Padre?"

"What do you mean?"

"The first step toward having Our Lady recognized as the incarnation of the feminine face of God? After all, we already accept the fact that Jesus was the incarnation of His masculine side."

"And so . . . ?"

"How much time must pass before we accept a Holy Trinity that includes a woman? The Trinity of the Holy Spirit, the Mother, and the Son?"

"Let's move on. It's too cold for us to stand here," he said. "A little while ago, you noticed my sandals."

"Have you been reading my mind?" I asked.

"I'm going to tell you part of the story of the founding of our religious order," he said. "We are barefoot Carmelites, according to the rules established by Saint Teresa of Avila. The sandals are a part of the story, for if one can dominate the body, one can dominate the spirit.

"Teresa was a beautiful woman, placed by her father in a convent so that she would receive a pure education. One day, when she was walking along a corridor, she began to speak with Jesus. Her ecstasies were so strong and deep that she surrendered totally to them, and in a short time, her life had been completely changed. She felt that the Carmelite convents had become nothing more than marriage brokerages, and she decided to create an order that would once again follow the original teachings of Christ and the Carmelites.

"Saint Teresa had to conquer herself, and she had to confront the great powers of her day—the church and the state. But she was determined to press on, because she was convinced that she had a mission to perform.

"One day—just when Teresa felt her soul to be weakening—a woman in tattered clothing appeared at the house where she was staying. The woman wanted to speak with Teresa, no matter what. The owner of the house offered the woman some alms, but the woman refused them; she would not go away until she had spoken with Teresa.

"For three days, the woman waited outside the house, without eating or drinking. Finally Teresa, out of sympathy, bade the woman come in.

" 'No,' said the owner of the house. 'The woman is mad.'

" 'If I were to listen to everyone, I'd wind up thinking that I'm the crazy one,' Teresa answered. 'It may be that this woman has the same kind of madness as I: that of Christ on the cross.' "

"Saint Teresa spoke with Christ," I said.

"Yes," he answered. "But to get back to our story: the woman was brought to Teresa. She said that her name was María de Jesus Yepes and that she was from Granada. She was a Carmelite novice, and the Virgin had appeared and asked that she found a convent that followed the primitive rules of the order."

Like Saint Teresa, I thought.

"María de Jesus left the convent on the day of her vision and began walking barefoot to Rome. Her pilgrimage lasted two years—and for that entire period, she slept outdoors, in the heat and the cold, living on alms and the charity of others. It was a miracle that she made it. But it was an even greater miracle that she was received by Pope Pius IV. Because the pope, just like

María de Jesus, Teresa, and many others, was thinking of the same thing," he finished.

Just as Bernadette had known nothing of the Vatican's decision and the monkeys from the other islands couldn't have known about the experiment that was being conducted, so María de Jesus and Teresa knew nothing of what the other was planning.

Something was beginning to make sense to me.

We were now walking through a forest. With the fog all but gone, the highest tree branches, covered with snow, were receiving the first rays of the sun.

"I think I know where you're going with this, Padre."

"Yes. The world is at a point when many people are receiving the same order: 'Follow your dreams, transform your life, take the path that leads to God. Perform your miracles. Cure. Make prophecies. Listen to your guardian angel. Transform yourself. Be a warrior, and be happy as you wage the good fight. Take risks.'"

Sunshine was everywhere. The snow was glistening, and the glare hurt my eyes. Yet at the same time, it seemed to support what the priest was saying.

"And what does all this have to do with him?"

"I've told you the heroic side of the story. But you don't know anything about the soul of these heroes."

He paused.

"The suffering," he picked up again. "At moments of transformation, martyrs are born. Before a person can follow his dream, others have to make sacrifices. They have to confront ridicule, persecution, and attempts to discredit what they are trying to do."

"It was the church that burned the witches at the stake, Padre."

"Right. And Rome threw the Christians to the lions. But those who died at the stake or in the sand of the arena rose quickly to eternal glory—they were better off.

"Nowadays, warriors of the light confront something worse than the honorable death of the martyrs. They are consumed, bit by bit, by shame and humiliation. That's how it was with Saint Teresa—who suffered for the rest of her life. That's how it was for María de Jesus, too. And for the happy children who saw Our Lady in Fátima, Portugal—well, Jacinta and Francisco died just a few months later; Lucia entered a convent from which she never emerged."

"But that's not how it was for Bernadette."

"Yes, it was. She had to live through prison, humiliation, and discredit. He must have described that to you. He must have told you the words of the visitation."

"Some of them."

"In the visitations at Lourdes, the phrases uttered by Our Lady wouldn't fill half a page of a notebook, but one of the things the Virgin said clearly to the girl was *'I do not promise you happiness in this world.'* Why did she warn Bernadette? Because she knew the pain that awaited Bernadette if she accepted her mission."

I looked at the sun, the snow, and the bare branches of the trees.

"He is a revolutionary," he continued, sounding humble. "He has the power, and he converses with Our Lady. If he is able to concentrate his forces well, he can be one of the leaders in the spiritual transformation of the human race. This is a critical point in the history of the world.

"But if he chooses this path, he is going to go through a great deal of suffering. His revelations have come to him before their time. I know the human soul well enough to know what he can expect."

The padre turned to me and held me by the shoulders. "Please," he said. "Keep him from the suffering and tragedy that lie in store for him. He will not be able to survive them."

"I understand your love for him, Padre."

He shook his head. "No, no. You don't understand anything. You are still too young to know the evils of the world. At this point, you see yourself as a revolutionary too. You want to change the world with him, open new paths, see the story of your love for each other become legend—a story passed down through the generations. You still think that love can conquer all."

"Well, can't it?"

"Yes, it can. But it conquers at the right time—after the celestial battles have ended."

"But I love him. I don't have to wait for the celestial battles to end for my love to win out."

He gazed into the distance.

"On the banks of the rivers of Babylon, we sat down and wept," he said, as if talking to himself. "On the willows there, we hung up our harps."

"How sad," I answered.

"Those are the first lines of one of the psalms. It tells of exile and of those who want to return to the promised land but cannot. And that exile is still going to last for a long time. What can I do to try to prevent the suffering of someone who wants to return to paradise before it is time to do so?"

"Nothing, Padre. Absolutely nothing."

(9 (9 (9

"THERE HE IS," said the padre.

I saw him. He was about two hundred yards from me, kneeling in the snow. He was shirtless, and even from that distance, I could see that his skin was red with the cold.

His head was bowed and his hands joined in prayer. I don't know if I was influenced by the ritual I had attended the night before or by the woman who had been gathering hay, but I felt that I was looking at someone with an incredible spiritual force. Someone who was no longer of this world—who lived in communion with God and with the enlightened spirits of heaven. The brilliance of the snow seemed to strengthen this perception.

"At this moment, there are others like him," said the priest. "In constant adoration, communing with God and the Virgin. Hearing the angels, the saints, the prophecies and words of wisdom, and transmitting all of that to a small gathering of the faithful. As long as they continue in this way, there won't be a problem.

"But he is not going to remain here. He is going to travel the world, preaching the concept of the Great Mother. The church is not yet ready for that. And the world has stones at hand to hurl at those who first introduce the subject."

"And it has flowers to throw on those who come afterward."

"Yes. But that's not what will happen to him."

The priest began to approach him.

"Where are you going?"

"To bring him out of his trance. To tell him how much I like you. To say that I give my blessing to your union. I want to do that here, in this place, which for him is sacred."

I began to feel sick with an inexplicable fear.

"I have to think, Padre. I don't know if this is right."

"It's not right," he answered. "Many parents make mistakes with their children, thinking they know what's best for them. I'm not his father, and I know I'm doing the wrong thing. But I have to fulfill my destiny."

I was feeling more and more anxious.

"Let's not disturb him," I said. "Let him finish his contemplation."

"He shouldn't be here. He should be with you."

"Maybe he's communicating with the Virgin."

"He may be. But even so, we have to go to him. If I approach him with you at my side, he will know that I have told you everything. He knows what I think."

"Today is the day of the Immaculate Conception," I insisted. "A very special day for him. I saw his happiness last night at the grotto."

"The Immaculate Conception is special for all of us," the padre answered. "But now I'm the one who doesn't want to discuss religion. Let's go to him."

"Why now, Padre? Why at this moment?"

"Because I know that he is deciding his future. And he may make the wrong choice."

I turned away and began to walk down the same path we had just come up. The padre followed me.

"What are you doing? Don't you see that you're the only one who can save him? Don't you see that he loves you and would give up everything for you?"

I hurried my steps, and it was difficult for him to keep up. Yet he fought to stay at my side.

"At this very moment, he is making his decision! He may be deciding to leave you! Fight for the person you love!"

But I didn't stop. I walked as fast as I could, trying to escape the mountains, the priest, and the choices behind me. I knew that the man who was rushing along behind me was reading my thoughts and that he understood that it was useless to try to make me go back. Yet he insisted; he argued and struggled to the end.

Finally, we reached the boulder where we had rested a half hour earlier. Exhausted, I threw myself down.

I tried to relax. I wanted to run from there, to be alone, to have time to think.

The padre appeared a few minutes later, as exhausted as I was.

"Do you see these mountains surrounding us?" he started in. "They don't pray; they are already a part of God's prayers. They have found their place in the world, and here they will stay. They were here before people looked to the heavens, heard thunder, and wondered who had created all of this. We are born, we suffer, we die, and the mountains endure.

"There is some point at which we have to wonder whether all our effort is worth it. Why not try to be like those mountains—wise, ancient, and in their place? Why risk everything to transform a half-dozen people who will immediately forget what they've been taught and move on to the next adventure? Why not wait until a certain number of monkeys learn, and then the knowledge will spread, with no suffering, to all the other islands?"

"Is that what you really think, Padre?"

He was silent for a few moments.

"Are you reading my thoughts now?"

"No. But if that's the way you feel, you wouldn't have chosen the religious life."

"I've tried many times to understand my fate," he said. "But I haven't yet. I accepted that I was to be a part of God's army, and everything I've done has been in an attempt to explain to people why there is misery, pain, and injustice. I ask them to be good Christians, and they ask me, 'How can I believe in God when there is so much suffering in the world?'

"And I try to explain something that has no explanation. I try to tell them that there is a plan, a battle among the angels, and that we are all involved in the battle. I try to say that when a certain number of people have enough faith to change the scenario, all of the others—everywhere on the planet—will benefit. But they don't believe me. They do nothing."

"They are like the mountains," I said. "The mountains are beautiful. Anyone who beholds them has to think about the grandness of creation. They are living proof of the love that God feels for us, but their fate is merely to give testimony. They are not like the rivers, which move and transform what is around them."

"Yes. But why not be like the mountains?"

"Maybe because the fate of mountains is terrible," I answered. "They are destined to look out at the same scene forever."

The padre said nothing.

"I was studying to become a mountain," I continued. "I had put everything in its proper place. I was going to take a job with the state, marry, and teach the religion of my parents to my children, even though I no longer accepted it. But now I have decided to leave all that behind me in order to be with the man I love. And it's a good thing I decided not to be a mountain—I wouldn't have lasted very long."

"You say some very wise things."

"I'm surprising myself. Before, all I could talk about was my childhood."

I stood and started back down the trail. The padre seemed to respect my silence and did not try to speak to me until we reached the road.

I took his hands and kissed them. "I'm going to say good-bye. But I want you to know that I understand you and your love for him."

The padre smiled and gave me his blessing. "And I understand your love for him, too," he said.

I spent the rest of the day walking through the valley. I played in the snow, visited a village near Saint-Savin, had a sandwich, and watched some boys playing soccer.

At the church in the village, I lit a candle. I closed my eyes and repeated the invocations I had learned the previous night. Then, concentrating on a crucifix that hung behind the altar, I began to speak in tongues. Bit by bit, the gift took over. It was easier than I had thought.

Perhaps this all seems silly—murmuring things, saying words that have no meaning, that don't help us in our reasoning. But when we do this, the Holy Spirit is conversing with our souls, saying things the soul needs to hear.

When I felt that I was sufficiently purified, I closed my eyes and prayed.

Our Lady, give me back my faith. May I also serve as an instrument of your work. Give me the opportunity to learn through my love, because love has never kept anyone away from their dreams.

May I be a companion and ally of the man I love. May we ac-complish everything we have to accomplish——together.

When I returned to Saint-Savin, night had almost fallen. The car was parked in front of the house where we were staying.

"Where have you been?" he asked.

"Walking and praying," I answered.

He embraced me.

"At first, I was afraid you had gone away. You are the most precious thing I have on this earth."

"And you are for me," I answered.

(∫ (∫ (∫

IT WAS LATE when we stopped in a small village near San Martín de Unx. Crossing the Pyrenees had taken longer than we'd thought because of the rain and snow of the previous day.

"We need to find someplace that's open," he said, climbing out of the car. "I'm hungry."

I didn't move.

"Come on," he insisted, opening my door.

"I want to ask you a question—a question I haven't asked since we found each other again."

He became serious, and I laughed at his concern.

"Is it an important question?"

"Very important," I answered, trying to look serious. "It's the following: where are we going?"

We both laughed.

"To Zaragoza," he said, relieved.

I jumped out of the car, and we went looking for a restaurant that was open. It was going to be almost impossible at that hour of the night.

No, it's not impossible. The Other is no longer with me. Miracles do happen, I said to myself. "When do you have to be in Barcelona?" I asked him. He'd told me he had another conference there.

He didn't answer, and his expression turned serious.

I shouldn't ask such questions, I thought. *He may think I'm trying to control his life.*

We walked along without speaking. In the village plaza, there was an illuminated sign: *Mesón el Sol.*

"It's open—let's have something to eat" was all he said.

The red peppers with anchovies were arranged on the plate in the shape of a star. On the side, some *manchego* cheese, in slices that were almost transparent. In the center of the table, a lighted candle and a half-full bottle of Rioja wine.

"This was a medieval wine cellar," our waiter told us.

There was no one in the place at that time of night. He went off to make a telephone call. When he came back to the table, I wanted to ask him whom he had called—but this time I controlled myself.

"We're open until two-thirty in the morning," the man said. "So if you like, we can bring you some more ham, cheese, and wine, and you can go out in the plaza. The wine will keep you warm."

"We won't be here that long," he answered. "We have to get to Zaragoza before dawn."

The man returned to the bar, and we refilled our glasses. I felt the same sense of lightness I had experienced in Bilbao—the smooth inebriation that helps us to say and hear things that are difficult.

"You're tired of driving, and we've been drinking," I said. "Wouldn't it be better to stay the night? I saw an inn as we were driving."

He nodded in agreement.

"Look at this table," he said. "The Japanese call it *shibumi*, the true sophistication of simple things. Instead, people fill their bank accounts with money and travel to expensive places in order to feel they're sophisticated."

I had some more wine.

The inn. Another night at his side.

"It's strange to hear a seminarian speak of sophistication," I said, trying to focus on something else.

"I learned about it at the seminary. The closer we get to God through our faith, the simpler He becomes. And the simpler He becomes, the greater is His presence.

"Christ learned about his mission while he was cutting wood and making chairs, beds, and cabinets. He came as a carpenter to show us that—no matter what we do—everything can lead us to the experience of God's love."

He stopped suddenly.

"But I don't want to talk about that," he said. "I want to talk about the other kind of love."

He reached out to caress my face. The wine made things easier for him. And for me.

"Why did you stop so suddenly? Why don't you want to talk about God and the Virgin and the spiritual world?"

"I want to talk about the other kind of love," he said again. "The love that a man and a woman share, and in which there are also miracles."

I took his hands. He might know of the great mysteries of the Goddess, but he didn't know any more than I did about love—even though he had traveled much more than I had.

We held hands for a long time. I could see in his eyes the deep fears that true love tests us with. I could see that he was remembering the rejection of the night before, as well as the long time we had been separated, and his years in the monastery, searching for a world where such anxieties didn't intrude.

I could see in his eyes the thousands of times that he had imagined this moment and the scenes he had constructed about us. I wanted to say that yes, he was welcome, that my heart had won the battle. I wanted to tell him how much I loved him and how badly I wanted him at that moment.

But I was silent. I witnessed, as if in a dream, his inner conflict. I could see that he was wondering whether I'd reject him again, that he was thinking about his fear of losing me, and about the hard words he had heard at other, similar times—because we all have such experiences, and they leave scars.

His eyes gleamed. He was ready to surmount any barrier.

I took one of my hands from his and placed my glass of wine at the edge of the table.

"It's going to fall," he said.

"Exactly. I want you to tip it over the edge."

"Break the glass?"

Yes, break the glass. A simple gesture, but one that brings up fears we can't really understand. What's wrong with breaking an inexpensive glass, when everyone has done so unintentionally at some time in their life?

"Break the glass?" he repeated. "Why?"

"Well, I could give you lots of reasons," I answered. "But actually, just to break it."

"For you?"

"No, of course not."

He eyed the glass on the edge of the table—worried that it might fall.

It's a rite of passage, I wanted to say. It's something prohibited. Glasses are not purposely broken. In a restaurant or in our home, we're careful not to place glasses by the edge of a table. Our universe requires that we avoid letting glasses fall to the floor.

But when we break them by accident, we realize that it's not very serious. The waiter says, "It's nothing," and when has anyone been charged for a broken glass? Breaking glasses is part of life and does no damage to us, to the restaurant, or to anyone else.

I bumped the table. The glass shook but didn't fall.

"Careful!" he said, instinctively.

"Break the glass," I insisted.

Break the glass, I thought to myself, *because it's a symbolic gesture. Try to understand that I have broken things within myself that were much more important than a glass, and I'm happy I did. Resolve your own internal battle, and break the glass.*

Our parents taught us to be careful with glasses and with our bodies. They taught us that the passions of childhood are impossible, that we should not flee from priests, that people cannot perform miracles, and that no one leaves on a journey without knowing where they are going.

Break the glass, please—and free us from all these damned rules, from needing to find an explanation for everything, from doing only what others approve of.

"Break the glass," I said again.

He stared at me. Then, slowly, he slid his hand along the tablecloth to the glass. And with a sudden movement, he pushed it to the floor.

The sound of the breaking glass caught the waiter's attention. Rather than apologize for having broken the glass, he looked at me, smiling—and I smiled back.

"Doesn't matter," shouted the waiter.

But he wasn't listening. He had stood, seized my hair in his hands, and was kissing me.

I clutched at his hair, too, and squeezed him with all my strength, biting his lips and feeling his tongue move in my mouth. This was the kiss I had waited for so long—a kiss born by the rivers of our childhood, when we didn't yet know what love meant. A kiss that had been suspended in the air as we grew, that had traveled the world in the souvenir of a medal, and that had remained hidden behind piles of books. A kiss that had been lost so many times and now was found. In the moment of that kiss were years of searching, disillusion-ment, and impossible dreams.

I kissed him hard. The few people there in the bar must have been thinking that all they were seeing was just a kiss. They didn't know that this kiss stood for my whole life—and his life, as well. The life of anyone who has waited, dreamed, and searched for their true path.

The moment of that kiss contained every happy moment I had ever lived.

ʕ ʕ ʕ

HE TOOK OFF MY CLOTHES and entered me with strength, with fear, and with great desire. I ran my hands over his face, heard his moans, and thanked God that he was there inside me, making me feel as if it were the first time.

We made love all night long—our lovemaking blended with our sleeping and dreaming. I felt him inside me and embraced him to make sure that this was really happening, to make sure that he wouldn't disappear, like the knights who had once inhabited this old castle-hotel. The silent walls of stone seemed to be telling stories of damsels in distress, of fallen tears and endless days at the window, looking to the horizon, looking for a sign of hope.

But I would never go through that, I promised myself. I would never lose him. He would always be with me—because I had heard the tongues of the Holy Spirit as I looked at a crucifix behind an altar, and they had said that I would not be committing a sin.

I would be his companion, and together we would tame a world that was going to be created anew. We would talk about the Great Mother, we would fight at the side of Michael the Archangel, and we would experience together the agony and the ecstasy of pioneers. That's what the tongues had said to me—and because I had recovered my faith, I knew they were telling the truth.

Thursday, December 9, 1993

❧ ❧ ❧

I AWOKE WITH HIS arm across my breast. It was already midmorning, and the bells of a nearby church were tolling.

He kissed me. His hands once again caressed my body.

"We have to go," he said. "The holiday ends today, and the roads will be jammed."

"I don't want to go back to Zaragoza," I answered. "I want to go straight to where you're going. The banks will be open soon, and I can use my bank card to get some money and buy some clothes."

"You told me you didn't have much money."

"There are things I can do. I need to break with my past once and for all. If we go back to Zaragoza,

I might begin to think I'm making a mistake, that the exam period is almost here and we can stand to be separated for two months until my exams are over. And then if I pass my exams, I won't want to leave Zaragoza. No, no, I can't go back. I need to burn the bridges that connect me with the woman I was."

"Barcelona," he said to himself.

"What?"

"Nothing. Let's move on."

"But you have a presentation to make."

"But that's two days from now," he said. His voice sounded different. "Let's go somewhere else. I don't want to go straight to Barcelona."

I got out of bed. I didn't want to focus on problems. As always after a first night of love with someone, I had awakened with a certain sense of ceremony and embarrassment.

I went to the window, opened the curtains, and looked down on the narrow street. The balconies of the houses were draped with drying laundry. The church bells were ringing.

"I've got an idea," I said. "Let's go to a place we shared as children. I've never been back there."

"Where?"

"The monastery at Piedra."

As we left the hotel, the bells were still sounding, and he suggested that we go into a church nearby.

"That's all we've done," I said. "Churches, prayers, rituals."

"We made love," he said. "We've gotten drunk three times. We've walked in the mountains. We've struck a good balance between rigor and compassion."

I'd said something thoughtless. I had to get used to this new life.

"I'm sorry," I said.

"Let's just go in for a few minutes. The bells are a sign."

He was right, but I wouldn't know that until the next day.

Afterward, without really understanding the meaning of the sign we had witnessed in the church, we got the car and drove for four hours to get to the monastery at Piedra.

(੭ (੭ (੭

THE ROOF HAD FALLEN in, and the heads were missing from the few images that were still there—all except for one.

I looked around. In the past, this place must have sheltered strong-willed people, who'd seen to it that every stone was cleaned and that each pew was occupied by one of the powerful individuals of the time.

But all I saw now were ruins. When we had played here as children, we'd pretended these ruins were castles. In those castles I had looked for my enchanted prince.

For centuries, the monks of the monastery at Piedra had kept this small piece of paradise to themselves. Situated on a valley floor, it enjoyed a plentiful supply of what the neighboring villages had to beg for—water. Here the River Piedra broke up into dozens of waterfalls, streams, and lakes, creating luxuriant vegetation all around.

Yet one had only to walk a few hundred yards to leave the canyon and find aridity and desolation. The river itself once again became a narrow thread of water—as if it had exhausted all of its youth and energy in crossing the valley.

The monks knew all this, and they charged dearly for the water they supplied to their neighbors. An untold number of battles between the priests and the villagers marked the history of the monastery.

During one of the many wars that shook Spain, the monastery at Piedra had been turned into a barracks. Horses rode through the central nave of the church, and soldiers slept in its pews, telling ribald stories there and making love with women from the neighboring villages.

Revenge—although delayed—finally came. The monastery was sacked and destroyed.

The monks were never able to reconstruct their paradise. In one of the many legal battles that followed, someone said that the inhabitants of the nearby villages had carried out a sentence pronounced by God. Christ had said, "Give drink to those who thirst," and the priests had paid no heed. For this, God had expelled those who had regarded themselves as nature's masters.

And it was perhaps for this reason that although much of the monastery had been rebuilt and made into a hotel, the main church remained in ruins. The descendants of the local villagers had never forgotten the high price that their parents had paid for something that nature provides freely.

"Which statue is that? The only one with its head?" I asked him.

"Saint Teresa of Avila," he answered. "She is power-ful. And even with the thirst for vengeance that the wars brought about, no one dared to touch her."

He took my hand, and we left the church. We walked along the broad corridors of the monastery, climbed the wooden staircases, and marveled at the butterflies in the inner gardens. I recalled every detail of that monastery because I had been there as a girl, and the old memories seemed more vivid than what I was seeing now.

Memories. The months and years leading up to that week seemed to be part of some other incarnation of mine—an era to which I never wanted to return, because it hadn't been touched by the hand of love. I felt as if I had lived the same day over and over for years on end, waking up every morning in the same way, repeating the same words, and dreaming the same dreams.

I remembered my parents, my grandparents, and many of my old friends. I recalled how much time I had spent fighting for something I didn't even want.

Why had I done that? I could think of no explana-tion. Maybe because I had been too lazy to think of other avenues to follow. Maybe because I had been afraid of what others would think. Maybe because it was hard work to be different. Perhaps because a human being is condemned to repeat the steps taken by the previous generation until—and I was thinking of the padre—a certain number of people begin to behave in a different fashion.

Then the world changes, and we change with it.

But I didn't want to be that way anymore. Fate had returned to me what had been mine and now offered me the chance to change myself and the world.

I thought again of the mountain climbers we had met as we traveled. They were young and wore brightly colored clothing so as to be easily spotted should they become lost in the snow. They knew the right path to follow to the peaks.

The heights were already festooned with aluminum pins; all they had to do was attach their lines to them, and they could climb safely. They were there for a holiday adventure, and on Monday they would return to their jobs with the feeling that they had challenged nature—and won.

But this wasn't really true. The adventurous ones were those who had climbed there first, the ones who had found the routes to the top. Some, who had fallen to their death on the rocks, had never even made it halfway up. Others had lost fingers and toes to frostbite.

Many were never seen again. But one day, some of them had made it to the summit.

And their eyes were the first to take in that view, and their hearts beat with joy. They had accepted the risks and could now honor—with their conquest—all of those who had died trying.

There were probably some people down below who thought, "There's nothing up there. Just a view. What's so great about that?"

But the first climber knew what was great about it: the acceptance of the challenge of going forward. He knew that no single day is the same as any other and that each morning brings its own special miracle, its *magic moment* in which ancient universes are destroyed and new stars are created.

The first one who climbed those mountains must have asked, looking down at the tiny houses with their smoking chimneys, "All of their days must seem the same. What's so great about that?"

Now all the mountains had been conquered and astronauts had walked in space. There were no more islands on earth—no matter how small—left to be discovered. But there were still great adventures of the spirit, and one of them was being offered to me now.

It was a blessing. The padre didn't understand anything. These pains are not the kind that hurt.

Fortunate are those who take the first steps. Someday people will realize that men and women are capable of speaking the language of the angels—that all of us are possessed of the gifts of the Holy Spirit and that we can perform miracles, cure, prophesy, and understand.

ᕱ ᕱ ᕱ

WE SPENT THE afternoon walking along the canyon, reminiscing about our childhood. It was the first time he had done so; during our trip to Bilbao, he had seemed to have lost all interest in Soria.

Now, though, he asked me about each of our mutual friends, wanting to know whether they were happy and what they were doing with their lives.

Finally, we arrived at the largest waterfall of the Piedra, where a number of small, scattered streams come together and the water is thrown to the rocks below from a height of almost one hundred feet. We stood at the edge of the waterfall, listening to its deafening roar and gazing at the rainbow in its mist.

"The Horse's Tail," I said, surprised that I still remembered this name from so long ago.

"I remember . . . ," he began.

"Yes! I know what you're going to say!"

Of course I knew! The waterfall concealed a gigantic grotto. When we were children, returning from our first visit to the monastery at Piedra, we had talked about that place for days.

"The cavern," he said. "Let's go there."

It was impossible to pass through the torrent of water. But ancient monks had constructed a tunnel that started at the highest point of the falls and descended through the earth to a place at the rear of the grotto.

It wasn't difficult to find the entrance. During the summer, there may even have been lights showing the way, but now the tunnel was completely dark.

"Is this the right way?" I asked.

"Yes. Trust me."

We began to descend through the hole at the side of the falls. Although we were in complete darkness, we knew where we were going—and he asked me again to trust him.

Thank you, Lord, I was thinking, as we went deeper and deeper into the earth, *because I was a lost sheep, and you brought me back. Because my life was dead, and you revived it. Because love wasn't alive in my heart, and you gave me back that gift.*

I held on to his shoulder. My loved one guided my steps through the darkness, knowing that we would see the light again and that it would bring us joy. Perhaps in our future there would be moments when the situation was reversed—when I would guide him with the same love and certainty until we reached a safe place and could rest together.

We walked slowly, and it seemed as if we would never stop descending. Maybe this was another rite of passage, marking the end of an era in which there had been no light in my life. As I walked through the tunnel, I was remembering how much time I had wasted in one place, trying to put down roots in soil where nothing could grow any longer.

But God was good and had given me back my lost enthusiasm, directing me toward the adventures I had always dreamed about. And toward the man who—without my knowing it—had waited for me all my life. I felt no remorse over the fact that he was leaving the seminary—there were many ways to serve God, as the padre had said, and our love only multiplied the number of them. Starting now, I would also have the chance to serve and help—all because of him.

We would go out into the world, bringing comfort to others and to each other.

Thank you, Lord, for helping me to serve. Teach me to be worthy of that. Give me the strength to be a part of his mission, to walk with him on this earth, and to develop my spiritual life anew. May all our days be as these have been—going from place to place, curing the sick, comforting those in sorrow, speaking of the Great Mother's love for all of us.

(9   (9   (9

SUDDENLY, THE SOUND of water could be heard again and light flooded our path. The dark tunnel was transformed into one of the most beautiful spectacles on earth. We were in an immense cavern, the size of a cathedral. Three of its walls were of stone, and the fourth was the Horse's Tail, with its water falling into the emerald-green lake at our feet.

The rays of the setting sun passed through the waterfall, and the moist walls glittered.

We leaned back against the stone wall, saying nothing.

When we were children, this place was a pirates' hideout, where the treasures of our childhood imagination were kept. Now, it was the miracle of Mother Earth; I knew she was there and felt myself to be in her womb. She was protecting us with her walls of stone and washing away our sins with her purifying water.

"Thank you," I said in a loud voice.

"Whom are you thanking?"

"Her. And you, because you were an instrument in restoring my faith."

He walked to the edge of the water. Looking out, he smiled. "Come over here," he said.

I joined him.

"I want to tell you something you don't know about yet," he said.

His words worried me a little. But he looked calm and happy, and that reassured me.

"Every person on earth has a gift," he began. "In some, the gift manifests itself spontaneously; others have to work to discover what it is. I worked with my gift during the four years I was at the seminary."

Now I would have to "play a role," as he had taught me when the old man had barred us from the church. I would have to feign that I knew nothing. *There's nothing wrong with doing this,* I told myself. *This is a not a script based on frustration but on happiness.*

"What did you do at the seminary?" I asked, trying to stall for time in order to play my role better.

"That doesn't matter," he said. "The fact is that I developed a gift. I am able to cure, when God so wills it."

"That's wonderful," I answered, acting surprised. "We won't have to spend money on doctors!"

He didn't laugh. I felt like an idiot.

"I developed my gift through the Charismatic practices that you saw," he went on. "In the beginning, I was surprised. I would pray, asking that the Holy Spirit appear, and then, through the laying on of my hands, I would restore many of the sick to good health. My reputation began to spread, and every day people lined up at the gates of the seminary, seeking my help. In every infected, smelly laceration, I saw the wounds of Jesus."

"I'm so proud of you," I said.

"Many of the people at the monastery opposed me, but my superior gave me his complete support."

"We'll continue this work. We'll go out together into the world. I will clean and bathe the wounds, and you will bless them, and God will demonstrate His miracles."

He looked away from me, out at the lake. There seemed to be a presence in the cavern similar to the one I had sensed that night in Saint-Savin when we had gotten drunk at the well in the plaza.

"I've already told you this, but I'll say it again," he continued. "One night I awoke, and my room was completely bright. I saw the face of the Great Mother; I saw Her loving look. After that, She began to appear to me from time to time. I cannot make it happen, but every once in a while, She appears.

"By the time of my first vision, I was already aware of the work being done by the true revolutionaries of the church. I knew that my mission on earth, in addition to curing, was to smooth the way for this new acceptance of God as a woman. The feminine principle, the column of Misericordia, would be rebuilt—and the temple of wisdom would be reconstructed in the hearts of all people."

I was staring at him. His face, which had grown tense, now relaxed again.

"This carried a price—which I was willing to pay."

He stopped, as if not knowing how to go on with his story.

"What do you mean when you say you *were* willing?" I asked.

"The path of the Goddess can only be opened through words and miracles. But that's not the way the world works. It's going to be very hard—tears, lack of understanding, suffering."

That padre, I thought to myself. *He tried to put fear in his heart. But I shall be his comfort.*

"The path isn't about pain; it's about the glory of serving," I answered.

"Most human beings still cannot trust love."

I felt that he was trying to tell me something but couldn't. I wanted to help him.

"I've been thinking about that," I broke in. "The first man who climbed the highest peak in the Pyrenees must have felt that a life without that kind of adventure would lack grace."

"What do you mean when you use the word *grace?*" he asked me, and I could see that he was feeling tense again. "One of the names of the Great Mother is Our Lady of the Graces. Her generous hands heap Her blessings on those who know how to receive them. We can never judge the lives of others, because each person knows only their own pain and renunciation. It's one thing to feel that you are on the right path, but it's another to think that yours is the only path.

"Jesus said, 'The house of my Father has many mansions.' A gift is a grace, or a mercy. But it is also a mercy to know how to live a life of dignity, love, and work. Mary had a husband on earth who tried to demonstrate the value of anonymous work. Although he was not heard from very much, he was the one who provided the roof over their heads and the food for their mouths, who allowed his wife and son to do all that they did. His work was as important as theirs, even though no one ever gave him much credit."

I didn't say anything, and he took my hand. "Forgive me for my intolerance."

I kissed his hand and put it to my cheek.

"This is what I'm trying to explain to you," he said, smiling again. "I realized, from the moment I found you again, that I couldn't cause you to suffer because of my mission."

I began to feel worried.

"Yesterday I lied to you. It was the first and last lie I've ever told you," he continued. "The truth is that instead of going to the monastery, I went up on the mountain and conversed with the Great Mother. I said to Her that if She wanted, I would leave you and continue along my path. I would go back to the gate where the sick gathered, to the visits in the middle of the night, to the lack of understanding of those who would deny the idea of faith, and to the cynical attitude of those who cannot believe that love is a savior. If She were to ask me, I would give up what I want most in the world: you."

I thought again of the padre. He had been right. A choice had been made that morning.

"But," he continued, "if it were possible to resolve this awful predicament in my life, I would promise to serve the world through my love for you."

"What are you saying?" I asked, frightened now.

He seemed not to hear me.

"It's not necessary to move mountains in order to prove one's faith," he said. "I was ready to face the suffering alone and not share it. If I had continued along that path, we would never have our house with the white curtains and the view of the mountains."

"I don't care about that house! I didn't even want to go in!" I said, trying not to shout. "I want to go with you, to be with you in your struggle. I want to be one of those who does something for the first time. Don't you understand? You've given me back my faith!"

The last rays of the sun illuminated the walls of the cavern. But I couldn't see its beauty.

God hides the fires of hell within paradise.

"You're the one who doesn't understand," he said, and I could see his eyes begging me to comprehend. "You don't see the risks."

"But you were willing to accept those risks!"

"I *am* willing. But they are *my* risks."

I wanted to interrupt him, but he wasn't listening.

"So yesterday, I asked a miracle of the Virgin," he continued. "I asked that She take away my gift."

I couldn't believe what I was hearing.

"I have a little money and all the experience that years of traveling have given me. We'll buy a house, I'll get a job, and I'll serve God as Saint Joseph did, with the humility of an anonymous person. I don't need miracles in my life anymore to keep the faith. I need you."

My legs were growing weak, and I felt as if I might faint.

"And just as I was asking that the Virgin take away my gift, I began to speak in tongues," he went on. "The tongues told me, 'Place your hands on the earth. Your gift will leave you and return to the Mother's breast.'"

I was in a panic. "You didn't . . ."

"Yes. I did as the inspiration of the Holy Spirit bade. The fog lifted, and the sun shone on the mountains. I felt that the Virgin understood—because She had also loved so greatly."

"But She followed Her man! She accepted the path taken by Her son!"

"We don't have Her strength, Pilar. My gift will be passed on to someone else—such gifts are never wasted.

"Yesterday, from that bar, I phoned Barcelona and canceled my presentation. Let's go to Zaragoza—you know the people there, and it's a good place for us to start. I'll get a job easily."

I could no longer think.

"Pilar!" he said.

But I was already climbing back through the tunnel—this time without a friendly shoulder to lean on—pursued by the multitude of the sick who would die, the families that would suffer, the miracles that would never be performed, the smiles that would no longer grace the world, and the mountains that would remain in place.

I saw nothing—only the darkness that engulfed me.

Friday, December 10, 1993

§ § §

ON THE BANK of the River Piedra I sat down and wept. My memory of that night is confused and vague. I know that I almost died, but I can't remember his face nor where he took me.

I'd like to be able to remember all of it—so that I could expel it from my heart. But I can't. It all seems like a dream, from the moment when I came out of that dark tunnel into a world where darkness had already fallen.

There was not a star in the sky. I remember vaguely walking back to the car, retrieving my small bag, and beginning to wander at random. I must have walked to the road, trying to hitch a ride to Zaragoza—with no success. I wound up returning to the gardens at the monastery.

The sound of water was everywhere—there were waterfalls on all sides, and I felt the presence of the Great Mother following me wherever I walked. Yes, She had loved the world; She loved it as much as God did—because She had also given Her son to be sacrificed by men. But did She understand a woman's love for a man?

She may have suffered because of love, but it was a different kind of love. Her Groom knew everything and performed miracles. Her husband on earth was a humble laborer who believed everything his dreams told him. She never knew what it was to abandon a man or to be abandoned by one. When Joseph considered expelling Her from their home because She was pregnant, Her Groom in heaven immediately sent an angel to keep that from happening.

Her son left Her. But children always leave their parents. It's easy to suffer because you love a person, or the world, or your son. That's the kind of suffering that you accept as a part of life; it's a noble, grand sort of suffering. It's easy to suffer for a cause or a mission; this ennobles the heart of the person suffering.

But how to explain suffering because of a man? It's not explainable. With that kind of suffering, a person feels as if they're in hell, because there is no nobility, no greatness—only misery.

That night, I slept on the frozen ground, and the cold anesthetized me. I thought I might die without a covering—but where could I find one? Everything that was most important in my life had been given so generously to me in the course of one week—and had been taken from me in a minute, without my having a chance to say a thing.

My body was trembling from the cold, but I hardly noticed. At some point, the trembling would stop. My body's energy would be exhausted from trying to provide me with heat and would be unable to do anything more. It would resume its customary state of relaxation, and death would take me in its arms.

I shook for another hour. And then peace came.

Before I closed my eyes, I began to hear my mother's voice. She was telling a story she had often told me when I was a child, not realizing it was a story about me.

"A boy and a girl were insanely in love with each other," my mother's voice was saying. "They decided to become engaged. And that's when presents are always exchanged.

"The boy was poor—his only worthwhile possession was a watch he'd inherited from his grandfather. Thinking about his sweetheart's lovely hair, he decided to sell the watch in order to buy her a silver barrette.

"The girl had no money herself to buy him a present. She went to the shop of the most successful merchant in the town and sold him her hair. With the money, she bought a gold watchband for her lover.

"When they met on the day of the engagement party, she gave him the wristband for a watch he had sold, and he gave her the barrette for the hair she no longer had."

❧ ❧ ❧

I WAS AWAKENED by a man shaking me.

"Drink this!" he was saying. "Drink this quickly!"

I had no idea what was happening nor the strength to resist. He opened my mouth and forced me to drink a hot liquid. I noticed that he was in his shirtsleeves and that he had given me a wrap.

"Drink more!" he insisted.

Without knowing what I was doing, I obeyed. Then I closed my eyes.

I awoke in the convent, and a woman was tending me.

"You almost died," she said. "If it weren't for the watchman, you wouldn't be here."

I stood up dizzily. Parts of the previous day came back to me, and I wished that the watchman had never passed my way.

But apparently this was not the time for me to die. I was to go on living.

The woman led me to the kitchen and prepared some coffee, biscuits, and bread for me. She asked me no questions, and I explained nothing. When I had finished eating, she gave me my bag.

"See if everything's still there," she said.

"I'm sure it is. I didn't really have anything much."

"You have your life, my child. A long life. Take better care of it."

"There's a city near here where there's a church," I said, wanting to cry. "Yesterday, before I came here, I went into that church with . . ."

I couldn't explain.

". . . with a friend from my childhood. I had already had enough of the churches around here, but the bells were ringing, and he said it was a sign—that we should go in."

The woman refilled my cup, poured some coffee for herself, and sat down to hear my story.

"We entered the church," I continued. "There was no one there, and it was dark. I tried to look for the sign, but I saw only the same old altars and the same old saints. Suddenly, we heard a movement above, where the organ was.

"It was a group of boys with guitars, who began to tune their instruments. We decided to sit and listen to the music for a while before continuing our trip. Shortly a man came in and sat down next to us. He was happy and shouted to the boys to play a *paso doble*."

"Bullfight music?" the woman said. "I hope they didn't do that!"

"They didn't. But they laughed and played a flamenco melody instead. My friend and I felt as if heaven had descended on us; the church, the surrounding darkness, the sound of the guitars, and the man's delight—it was all a miracle.

"Little by little, the church began to fill. The boys continued to play the flamenco, and everyone who came in smiled, infected by the joy of the musicians.

"My friend asked if I wanted to attend the mass that was about to begin. I said no—we had a long ride ahead of us. So we decided to leave—but before we did, we thanked God for yet another beautiful moment in our lives.

"As we arrived at the gate, we saw that many people —perhaps the entire population of the town—were walking to the church. I thought it must have been the last completely Catholic town in Spain—maybe because the crowds seemed to be having so much fun.

"As we got into the car, we saw a funeral procession approaching. Someone had died; it was a mass for the dead. As soon as the cortege reached the gates of the church, the musicians stopped the flamenco music and began to play a dirge."

"May God have mercy on that soul," said the woman, crossing herself.

"May He have mercy," I said, repeating her gesture. "But our having gone into that church really had been a sign—that every story has a sad ending."

The woman said nothing. Then she left the room and returned immediately with a pen and paper.

"Let's go outside," she said.

We went out together, and the sun was rising.

"Take a deep breath," she said. "Let this new morning enter your lungs and course through your veins. From what I can see, your loss yesterday was not an accident."

I didn't answer.

"You also didn't really understand the story you told me, about the sign in the church," she went on. "You saw only the sadness of the procession at the end. You forgot the happy moments you spent inside. You forgot the feeling that heaven had descended on you and how good it was to be experiencing all of that with your . . ."

She stopped and smiled.

". . . childhood friend," she said, winking. "Jesus said, 'Let the dead bury the dead' because he knew that there is no such thing as death. Life existed before we were born and will continue to exist after we leave this world."

My eyes filled with tears.

"It's the same with love," she went on. "It existed before and will go on forever."

"You seem to know everything about my life," I said.

"All love stories have much in common. I went through the same thing at one point in my life. But that's not what I remember. What I remember is that love returned in the form of another man, new hopes, and new dreams."

She held out the pen and paper to me.

"Write down everything you're feeling. Take it out of your soul, put it on the paper, and then throw it away. Legend says that the River Piedra is so cold that anything that falls into it—leaves, insects, the feathers of birds—is turned to stone. Maybe it would be a good idea to toss your suffering into its waters."

I took the pages. She kissed me, and said I could come back for lunch if I wanted to.

"Don't forget!" she shouted as she walked away. "Love perseveres. It's men who change."

I smiled, and she waved good-bye.

I looked out at the river for some time. And I cried until there were no more tears.

Then I began to write.

Epilogue

❧ ❧ ❧

I wrote for an entire day, and then another, and another. Every morning, I went to the bank of the River Piedra. Every afternoon, the woman came, took me by the arm, and led me back to the old convent.

She washed my clothes, made me dinner, chatted about trivial things, and sent me to bed.

One morning, when I had almost finished the manuscript, I heard the sound of a car. My heart leaped, but I didn't want to believe it. I felt free again, ready to return to the world and be a part of it once again.

The worst had passed, although the sadness remained.

But my heart was right. Even without raising my eyes from my work, I felt his presence and heard his footsteps.

"Pilar," he said, sitting down next to me.

I went on writing, without answering. I couldn't pull my thoughts together. My heart was jumping, trying to free itself from my breast and run to him. But I wouldn't allow it.

He sat there looking at the river, while I went on writing. The entire morning passed that way—without a word—and I recalled the silence of a night near a well when I'd suddenly realized that I loved him.

When my hand could write no longer, I stopped. Then he spoke.

"It was dark when I came up out of the cavern. I couldn't find you, so I went to Zaragoza. I even went to Soria. I looked everywhere for you. Then I decided to return to the monastery at Piedra to see if there was any sign of you, and I met a woman. She showed me where you were, and she said you had been waiting for me."

My eyes filled with tears.

"I am going to sit here with you by the river. If you go home to sleep, I will sleep in front of your house. And if you go away, I will follow you—until you tell me to go away. Then I'll leave. But I have to love you for the rest of my life."

I could no longer hold back the tears, and he began to weep as well.

"I want to tell you something . . . ," he started to say.

"Don't say a thing. Read this." I handed him the pages.

♔   ♔   ♔

I GAZED AT THE RIVER PIEDRA all afternoon. The woman brought us sandwiches and wine, commented on the weather, and left us alone. Every once in a while, he paused in his reading and stared out into space, absorbed in his thoughts.

At one point I went for a walk in the woods, past the small waterfalls, through the landscape that was so laden with stories and meanings for me. When the sun began to set, I went back to the place where I had left him.

"Thank you" was what he said as he gave the papers back to me. "And forgive me."

On the bank of the River Piedra, I sat down and wept.

"Your love has saved me and returned me to my dream," he continued.

I said nothing.

"Do you know Psalm 137?" he asked.

I shook my head. I was afraid to speak.

"On the banks of the rivers of Babylon . . ."

"Yes, yes, I know it," I said, feeling myself coming back to life, little by little. "It talks about exile. It talks about people who hang up their harps because they cannot play the music their hearts desire."

"But after the psalmist cries with longing for the land of his dreams, he promises himself,

If I forget you, O Jerusalem,
let my right hand forget its skill.
Let my tongue cling to the roof of my mouth,
if I do not exalt Jerusalem."

I smiled again.

"I had forgotten, and you brought it back to me."

"Do you think your gift has returned?" I asked.

"I don't know. But the Goddess has always given me a second chance in life. And She is giving me that with you. She will help me to find my path again."

"Our path."

"Yes, ours."

He took my hands and lifted me to my feet.

"Go and get your things," he said. "Dreams mean work."